CW01658886

Hang Glider Pilot

John Murray

Hang Glider Pilot

Ann Welch &
Gerry Breen

ALSO BY ANN WELCH

Pilots' Weather
The Story of Gliding (*with Lorne Welch*)
New Soaring Pilot (*with Lorne Welch and Frank Irving*)

Text set in 11/12 pt Photon Times, printed by photolithography, and bound in Great Britain at The Pitman Press, Bath

ISBN 0 7195 3377 5

Contents

Sources of Illustrations

The authors are grateful for permission to reproduce the following illustrations:

Adrian Turner, Zuidyk Studios, Brighton: title-page, 2.3, 5.1, 7.1, 8.1, 8.3, 9.2, 9.3, 9.4, 10.1, 10.2, 10.4, 10.5, 10.6, 11.2, 11.7, 11.8, 11.9, 12.3, 12.4, 13.1, 13.2, 13.4, 13.6, 17.1, 17.8

Henry Heggie, Strood: 11.3, 11.4, 11.5, 15.2

Kestrel Kites, South Poole: 7.2

Keystone Press Agency, London: 1.1

Leslie Lane, Burgess Hill: 14.2

Alan Nutten: 14.1

Photocall Features, London: 1.2

Otto Lilienthal (1848–96) built various hang gliders and made some 2,000 flights on them, many from a specially built hill.

INTRODUCTION

How it began

It is in some ways a pity that flying became possible at the start of this century, when industrial and engineering progress was moving fast. Technical advancement was the cry and the first simple products of the dream to fly were swept along being made better, faster, heavier, and more expensive as quickly as it was possible to create new designs. World War I, of course, gave a powerful stimulant to the infant flying machine. The original intention—to fly with the facility and beauty of the birds—mostly faded with the original pioneers. But it never entirely disappeared, remaining quietly there alongside the high-speed technology and the thrust for power. It took no great search to discover people who continued to believe in the individual challenge of flying, and in the unique and special attractiveness of soaring.

Some of these people became famous—like Wolf Hirth, who was the first to discover how to make real use of thermals. With aeroplanes, it was Geoffrey de Havilland and his Gipsy Moth who effectively opened up the world to migratory man. But there were others who flew unnoticed, following their dream. Few now have heard of Willi Pelzner who in 1911 built hang gliders out of scrap, to escape from school and go up into the hills to fly. But he did not manage to soar.

Lilienthal almost managed it. On the Rhinow hills in the 1890s he often rose above his starting-point, remaining hovering over the ground for a considerable time. He felt quite surely that he could fly further if he 'inclined a little to one side, made a circular movement, or let himself be driven by the wind'. But another twenty years were to pass before the German Fredric Harth soared for a little over 2 minutes above a slope in the Black Forest, and the way ahead became clear.

Ferdinand Schultz was a schoolteacher who lived on the shores of the Baltic, and passionately believed that he could fly all day long over the sand-dunes, the highest of which barely reached 200 ft. He built himself a primitive aircraft which would soar no better than a rogallo, and taught himself to find lift over the rolling sand. From his first 6 minutes in 1923 he went on to achieve over 8 hours, and later 9 hours with a passenger, on a somewhat better and stronger glider. By 1926 Uncle Ferdinand, as he was called, soared along the Baltic dunes to Memel, 36 miles away. Often his wingtip barely cleared the blowing sand while trying to extract lift out of some isolated gust. To cross gaps in the dunes he flew out over the sea to use the meagre lift provided by the windward side of heavy surf.

In England, Itford Hill was chosen as the site of the 1922 *Daily Mail* Competition, with £1,000 offered for the longest duration flight in a glider. This was won by the Frenchman Alex Maneyrol on a 21-ft span tandem wing glider, having a glide ratio of probably about 1:9. He stayed airborne for 3 hours 21 minutes 7 seconds, a world duration record.

After this only birds soared the South Downs for the next eight years, until Robert Kronfeld arrived from Germany in 1930 with his 63-ft span Wien. In these intervening years the performance of gliders had improved greatly, and wandering along the hills had become a reality (and is the next step for hang gliding). Kronfeld was to give demonstration flights at Itford, where the new Southdown Gliding Club had started, and he did so all that day. As the afternoon wore on he increasingly felt the urge to explore along the hills, but it was not until 5.30 p.m. that he could escape, and use the north-east wind as he wanted. He wrote later that unfortunately the wind was already dropping, with the air much cooler. The first minutes of the flight were used to gain as much height as he could over Firle Beacon, as before him was the problem of getting over the $2\frac{1}{2}$-mile valley to Cliffe Hill, north-east of Lewes. He lost height

Willi Pelzner and other enthusiasts constructed their hang gliders from scrap materials and flew from the Rhön mountains in Germany before and just after World War I.

Ferdinand Schultz's broomstick on which he soared over sand-dunes for 8 hrs 42 min in 1924.

gliding across, but after a few alarming minutes reached the ridge and began to climb; and in a strong upcurrent caused by 'the best soaring slope of the whole district' he quickly gained height and crossed over the next large valley north of Lewes to Mount Harry. He described how north of Brighton the Downs began to bend south, and how it was difficult to retain his height as the north-east wind was now blowing almost parallel to the slope. He managed to cross a further valley 3 miles wide—the Arun—but the slackening wind was making it more and more difficult to carry on. However, the flight along the ridge to Petersfield presented no real difficulty, but it was already past 8 p.m. and both the wind and the visibility were deteriorating rapidly. Kronfeld reckoned that it might just have been possible to reach Winchester had it not been so late, so he resolved to drift downwind to land at Portsmouth. To do this he had to stay airborne over substantially flat land 'with only a few hills and coppices to offer late upcurrents'. His chief difficulty was to find the place in the murk. Passing over the top of the last small hill that he could see near Petersfield he called out at the top of his voice 'Where's Portsmouth?' He saw a man below 'first turn around three times trying to find where the voice came from and at last look up. Then he pointed the direction.' Kronfeld cleared the top of Portsdown Hill by 15 ft, but then did not like the look of what he described as the swampy outskirts of the town, so turned back and landed on the hill itself at 8.30 p.m. In later years Itford and Firle were soared by gliders from the Southdown Club until it moved to Parham in 1973. Now hang gliders soar over these historic hills.

By the late 1920s performance was reaching out to glide angles of 1 : 20, and enthusiasm for new ideas was great. These gliding pioneers would have been delighted by the simplicity of the rogallo, fascinated by ultralights such as Icarus V and Tweetie, and awed by the incredible performance of the glass-fibre glider, now in sight of a glide ratio of 1 : 50. It is our good luck that out of the high-powered technology of 20th-century engineering progress has come a fantastic range of lightweight structural materials and probably the cheapest and most basic aircraft that it is possible to devise—the rogallo. Although the Chinese flew simple and elegantly designed kites more than a thousand years ago, and Leonardo da Vinci had enough knowledge to design a complex helicopter, no one developed the concept of the delta sailwing, even though suitable materials were available and the construction problem was negligible. Sir George Cayley probably came nearest to the rogallo solution with his 'Governable Parachute' the drawings for which were published in *Mechanics Magazine* of 25 September 1852. This aircraft was reputed to have been flown, unwillingly, by Cayley's coachman but nothing was certain until a replica was made a few years ago. It flew.

Almost certainly the reason why the rogallo was not invented many years before was that it needed a much more complete understanding of aerodynamics to achieve this answer. Early experimenters found it difficult to depart both structurally and in aerodynamic shape from the birds, which were the only examples of flying machines available to them. The original interest of Francis Rogallo and his wife was to develop totally flexible kites and they only later developed their ideas for the benefit of the American Space Program. Francis Rogallo started working for NASA in the forties and over the next few years filed some twenty patents, some jointly with his wife. In the sixties the new hang glider movement had its small beginnings, and inevitably some rogallo-shaped wings were built along with copies of 1920 hang gliders and other interesting devices. In 1972 Francis Rogallo took out another patent, this time to get earthbound man airborne instead of space capsules back to earth. Since then the sport has never looked back. The performance of the rogallo is minimal, but it works because it is so incredibly simple and light, because it is robust and cheap, and because it is the next best thing to growing one's own wings.

Full circle now, we have the aircraft, but the dream must not be lost again. The need for speed and sophistication is pretty well ingrained, and the temptation to build hang gliders that are fast, complicated, expensive, or even hung all over with electronics is lying in wait. It has to be resisted. The world is already full of magnificent sailplanes and aeroplanes that can provide almost any degree of sophistication and performance that a pilot could want—or pay for. Hang gliders can be improved, but they must stay light and simple. They are for the pure pleasure of personal flying; for the delights of soaring over beautiful hills.

The original of Sir George Cayler's 'Governable Parachute' flew in 1852. This exact replica was flown by Derek Piggott in 1974.

I GETTING STARTED

CHAPTER ONE

What is a hang glider and how does it fly?

About the rogallo

The ordinary delta-sailwing rogallo is a very simple flying machine. Constructed of aluminium tube made into a rigid structure by bracing wires, and covered with a lightweight synthetic material, the aircraft is cheap and easy to build. (Fig. 1.1.) But it is an aircraft and not a toy, and like any aircraft it is potentially lethal.

1.1. Rogallo with a seat harness. The pilot is in the neutral position with arms bent. This allows for freedom of fore and aft control.

1.2. Dragonfly. The longer, narrower, high aspect-ratio wing gives a better glide performance but requires more skill to fly. The windows help the pilot to see other hang gliders overhead.

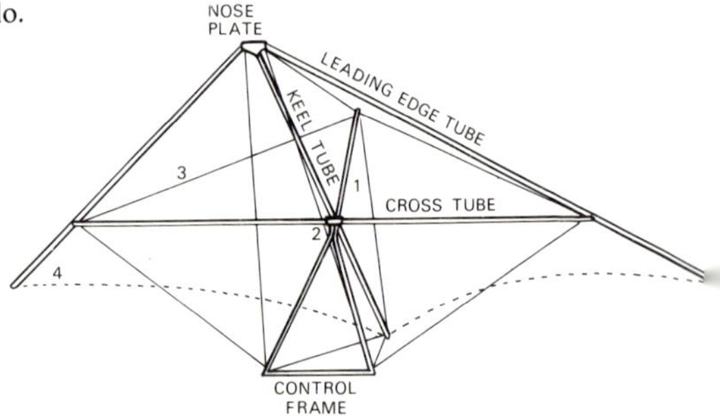

1.3. Structure of a rogallo.
(1) kingpost,
(2) heart bolt,
(3) bracing wires,
(4) dotted line shows
extent of sail.

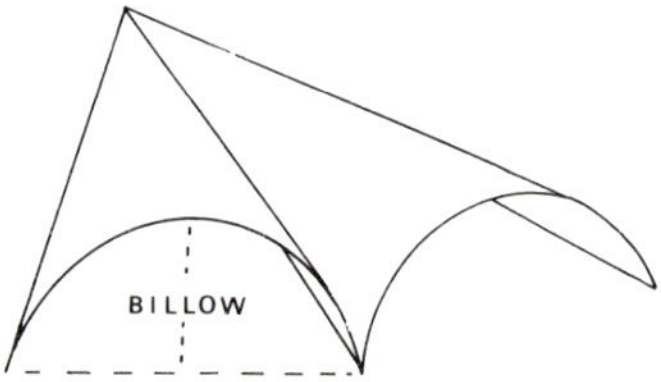

1.4. Billow. The sail billow is measured as the difference between the angle of the airframe and of the sail. In the example a 9° difference gives 4.5° of billow on each lobe.

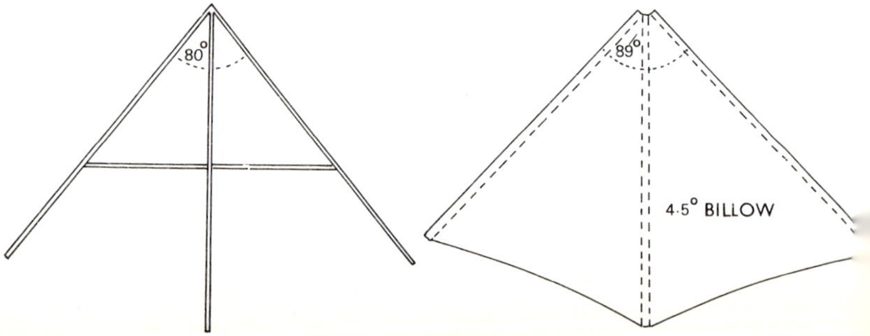

A hang glider may look simple and it is exhilarating and fun to fly, but as with other forms of aviation you may not have the chance to repeat a mistake.

There are many rogallo variants ranging from the original conical rogallo, by way of semi-cylindrical craft having curved leading-edge tubes, to 'second generation' hang gliders with longer high aspect-ratio wings and flatter cut sails. (Figs. 1.2–1.4.) There are also hang gliders shaped more like conventional aeroplanes—more about them in Chapter 17. All these hang gliders are different in flying characteristics and performance. Most people start their flying on one of the many standard rogallos on the market, which are robust, safe, and suitable for training. The high aspect-ratio hang gliders are more sensitive to control and should not be flown by inexperienced pilots.

Hang gliders are made in a range of sizes to cope with different weight pilots. A heavier pilot will need more wing area than a light one to achieve the same wing loading. This should be just under 1 lb/sq. ft for ordinary flying. The wing area is determined by the length of the two leading edge and the keel tubes, the angle at which they meet at the nose, and the amount of this basic triangular shape that is filled by the sail. The sail itself is not cut flat but with considerable curvature on each side of the keel tube, called the billow. Looked at in more detail leading edge tubes range from 14 ft to 20 ft on each side which permits sail areas from around 140 sq. ft to 280 sq. ft, typically 200 sq. ft. If a pilot flies a hang glider smaller in area than specified for his weight he will find that (a) it has a higher sinking speed, (b) it is more manoeuvrable, and (c) the stall speed will be higher. If, on the other hand, he flies a bigger, and therefore more lightly loaded hang glider than specified the effect will be (a) an improvement in sink rate, but (b) less control, because the span and mass of the aircraft is much greater in relation to the pilot weight. The recommendations of the manufacturer should be followed in choosing the size of wing that is best for your weight and the sort of flying you want to do. The nose angle is the angle at which the two leading edge tubes are set, and fixed by the cross member. Taking 90° as basic, angles greater than this slightly im-

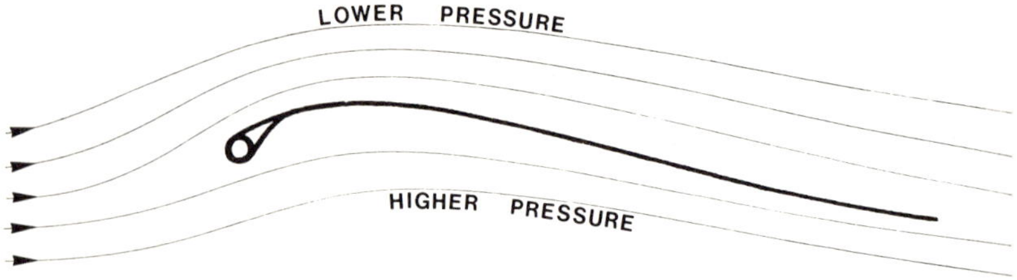

1.5. Simplified airflow past a rogallo wing. In reality, the flow is affected by imperfections of the sail, and by cross tube drag.

prove the performance at the price of poorer lateral control, while smaller angles, between 80° and 90° give quicker lateral response but not such a good performance. Angles of less than 80° are not practicable.

The sail billow is the amount of fullness given to the sail when the fabric is cut. (Fig. 1.5.) The greater the billow, within reason, the more directionally stable the aircraft and the gentler the stall at the price of some loss in performance, while flatter cut sails will perform slightly better but have less inherent stability. The billow amount is expressed as the additional angle in degrees for each half of the sail in relation to the nose angle. A rogallo used for training has 3–4° of billow. 4.5° or more makes the aircraft increasingly difficult to turn.

The wing area is the area measured between the leading edge tubes. It is the projected area of the sail, not the actual area of the material. The best material is terylene (dacron) at about 3.8 oz/sq. yd. Ripstop nylon is sometimes used but stretches easily so that the sail ripples and is noisy. Polythene can be used; it is cheap but hard to fix and easily damaged.

How a rogallo flies

No aircraft will fly unless there is a sufficiently fast airflow moving past the wing to cause it to lift. The rogallo wing is a single-surface flexible sail cut so that when it is filled, or inflated, by the airflow it will generate lift. The speed at which the airflow has to move past

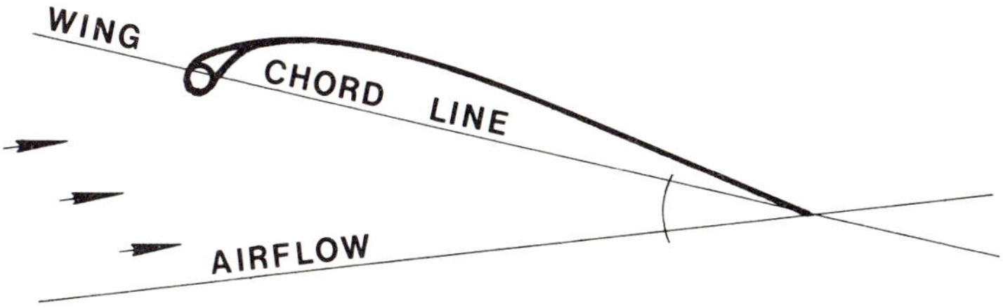

1.6. The angle of attack is the angle between the chord line of the wing and the angle of airflow.

the wing to enable a rogallo to fly is 15–18 mph. Below this speed the wing will not generate enough lift and will be partially stalled. (Fig. 1.6.) A hang glider can maintain its speed only with the aid of gravity. It is always gliding downhill, just as a bicycle maintains its speed when free wheeling down a hill.

Angle of attack

To inflate the sail and generate lift the wing has to meet the airflow at a positive angle, called the *angle of attack*. It has nothing to do with the angle of the wing to the horizon, or whether or not you are soaring.

Airspeed and groundspeed

When the airflow is moving past the wing sufficiently fast to generate enough lift the aircraft will have *flying speed*. It must continue to maintain this airspeed through the air all the time if it is to continue to fly. The airspeed is not the same as the speed over the ground, except on a completely calm day. The groundspeed will be altered by the strength of the wind and by whether the aircraft is being flown into or down wind. For example, if you are flying at an airspeed of 20 mph against a wind of 15 mph your headway over the ground will be only 5 mph. You can see this when hang gliders are soaring in a strong wind, and appear to be almost stationary.

Their airspeed through the air is equivalent to the strength of the wind into which they are heading. This is why it can be dangerous to turn downwind without a great deal of distance and height to spare. Immediately, your speed over the ground will be the airspeed of the rogallo *plus* the wind strength. This will change the speed over the ground from a walking speed of 3–4 mph to perhaps 40, even 60 mph!

The advantage of taking off into a wind instead of in calm air, is that while on the ground you have this bonus airflow moving past the wing and helping to inflate it. If you are facing into a wind of 10–12 mph you will need only to run at about 5 mph in order to achieve flying speed. If the wind is stronger at, say, 18–20 mph, only a couple of steps will be needed to get airborne. This is why you always take off into wind.

Once airborne, the necessary airspeed will be achieved and maintained by flying your hang glider at the proper angle of attack for normal flight. The rogallo will move forward over the ground if the wind strength is less than the airspeed of the rogallo, or backwards over the ground if the wind strength is greater than the airspeed. In this case the airspeed will have to be increased to penetrate into the wind and avoid being blown backwards into or over the top of the hill.

The stall

When speed is reduced the rogallo will fly at an increasingly large angle of attack, will lose airspeed and will eventually stall. If speed is reduced slowly the stall will develop in a much less well-defined manner than for a conventional aeroplane wing. This is because the airflow on the under surface of the sail at high angles of attack helps to keep it inflated. However, the rate of sink of the rogallo will be considerably increased if it is flown very slowly, producing a parachute-like descent.

If speed is reduced sharply, because the pilot has rapidly increased the angle of attack, the stall will be more clearly defined.

The airflow over the top surface of the wing which had become turbulent as the stall developed will now separate, and the nose will pitch down—perhaps sharply. You will not be able to prevent this. High aspect-ratio rogallos usually have a sharper stall.

Theory into practice

To get a feel for how a rogallo flies ask a pilot to show you the following, but not in a strong wind.

With someone lightly holding the nose wires, stand holding the rogallo facing into wind with the sail horizontal so that the fabric is flapping. The sail is not now providing lift. Raise the nose slowly and the flapping will decrease as the sail begins to fill and look like it does when it is in the air. The wing has now reached a positive angle of attack to the airflow. If it is only just filled this will be the minimum angle of attack at which the rogallo will fly. If the angle of attack is further increased the lift of the wing will increase, but so will the drag. You can feel this. Do not forget that drag goes up as the square of the speed—more about this later.

If the angle of attack is increased still further the drag will become greater, but the lift will now lessen as the airflow starts to become turbulent over the top surface. At this high angle of attack the wing will be partially stalled, and if the aircraft were in the air the sink rate would become high. Now slowly reduce the angle of attack again. The drag will be felt to decrease, and the lift increase as the sail becomes unstalled. As the angle of attack is reduced still further the lift will be felt to weaken as the sail ceases to remain properly filled. A further lowering of the nose will cause the sail to deflate and undulate noisily. The wing is now at a 'negative angle of attack' with the airflow passing equally over the top and bottom surfaces of the sail; insufficient lift exists to fly. The wing is now in the same state as a boat sail when it is luffed—pointing into wind with the sail flapping and providing no drive to the boat. The big difference between the boat and the rogallo is that the boat is already on the surface when its sail ceases to work. The rogallo is in the air and it may be a long way to the ground. If you luff your wing in the air you will have neither lift nor control, since there is now nothing for the pilot's weight shift to react against. This luffing condition, which is inherent in any flexible sailwing is extremely dangerous, because there is no practical means of preventing the aircraft diving into the ground.

In normal flight a properly designed, built, and rigged rogallo will not luff, the manufacturer having arranged that even with the pilot weight fully forward on the control frame, the dive will not be steep enough to cause the sail to collapse. But it is very important that you should know the circumstances in which it might occur. If you indulge in aerobatic-type flying, particularly stalling deliberately sharply, or if you fly in severe mountain turbulence with negative gusts, or if you lose control in a 360° turn by spiralling down far too fast, you risk luffing. You have to appreciate from the start that a rogallo is a simple, basic aircraft, and to accept that there is a limit to what it can do.

CHAPTER TWO

Hang glider control and performance

Weight shift control

A rogallo is controlled by shifting body weight in relation to the centre of gravity—or balance point—of the aircraft. The chapters on learning to fly tell how to do it, but briefly control is achieved by shifting or moving your weight in relation to the control frame. From the neutral position, seated comfortably with the arms bent, you pull your body weight forward towards the control frame to increase speed. Or if you want to turn right you move your body weight out to the right. (Fig. 2.1.)

So as to be able to have maximum freedom of movement the pilot has a swinging harness. This may position you in an upright position on a small seat or it may allow you to adopt a supine or prone position. (Fig. 2.2.) With the swing seat you remain at all

2.1. Control by weight shift. Pulling the body weight forward makes the nose pitch down and the aircraft fly faster. Pushing the body weight back pitches the nose up and reduces the speed.

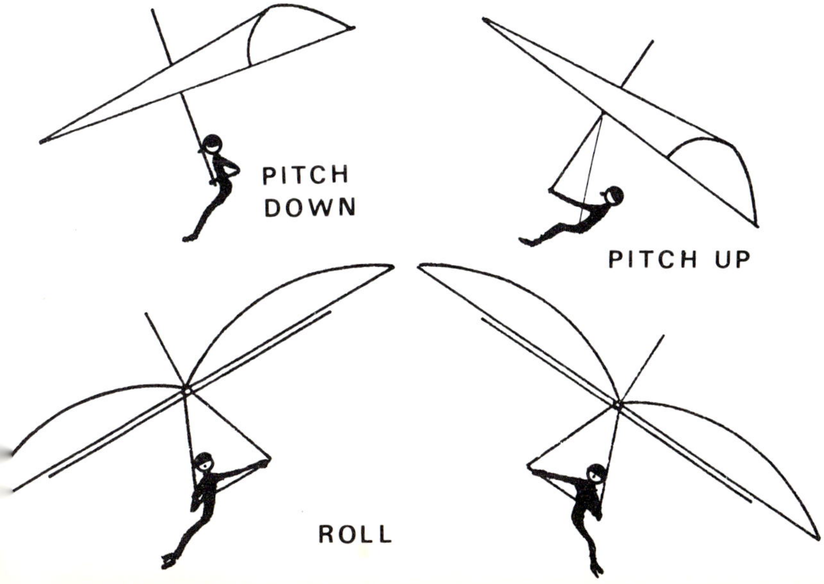

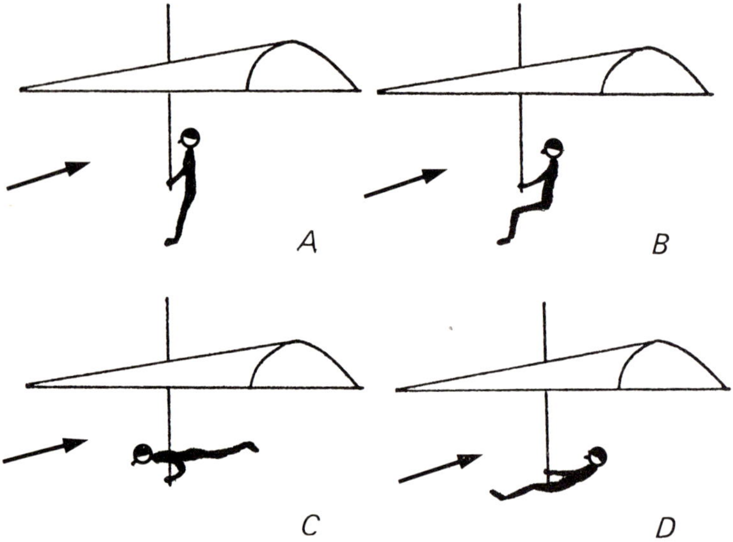

2.2. The drag of the pilot. (a) Vertical the pilot produces 10 sq. ft of drag. Seated (b) about 8 sq. ft, and prone (c) or supine (d) about 2 sq. ft.

times in the take-off or landing position, and have good control power because of the amount that you can swing your body about. The hang glider is stable because the pilot weight is low down like a pendulum, but the drag of the seated pilot is higher than when he is prone. The rogallo will neither accelerate nor soar so well, particularly in marginal conditions. With a prone or supine harness the pilot initially stands so that he can run to take off, and then swings himself horizontal, with his harness tether line running through a ring or pulley at the top of the control frame. For soaring knee hangers or a special harness are necessary so that the legs can be held in line with the body. Some pilots hitch their feet over the two bracing wires to the rear end of the keel to achieve a sort of prone position; this is extremely bad practice as it will not only distort the aircraft, but the pilot's boots may catch. Fatalities have occurred this way. Control with a prone harness demands skill and well-trained muscles so it is not normally used while learning. It can also be tiring on a long flight. A

2.3. Flying prone reduces drag, improving glide performance.

good harness allows the body to go naturally into the prone position, but minimum drag cannot be achieved unless the body is pointing into the actual airflow. This means that the feet will need to be kept well up. (Fig. 2.3.) Alternatively the pilot can fly supine. It is easier to achieve a better aerodynamic shape and is less tiring. However, the control range is less than prone.

Reflex and other adjustments

Slight adjustments can be made by the pilot to the curvature of the keel tube and the cross bar, by tightening and slackening the appropriate bracing wires. The keel tube is normally reflexed, or curved up towards the trailing edge in order to impart this shape to the sail. In a dive reflex will make the nose want to come up. If the nose is too high and the angle of attack great it causes the sail to stall slightly earlier than it would without reflex. The usual amount of reflex is very small, about 1–1½°, just enough to improve stability but not enough to noticeably affect the stall.

The cross tube can be curved slightly upwards towards the tips to give the wing a dihedral angle. In general dihedral increases lateral stability, although with the complex three-dimensional sail shape of the rogallo dihedral of the cross tube may in fact reduce the actual and effective dihedral of the outer parts of the wings. Dihedral would help the aircraft to fly straight but requires a little more effort to make it turn. In gusts it would help to return the aircraft to an even keel. Rogallos need little or no dihedral of the cross tube as they have considerable built-in lateral stability due to the position of the pilot well below the wing, as well as appreciable billow in the sail. Some dihedral may be more useful on higher aspect-ratio wings with flatter cut sails.

Some rogallos are fitted with leading edge wires, or deflexers, for maintaining the tubes straight under flight loads. They are not so necessary on training rogallos but for performance flying avoid the after end of the leading edge tubes bending in and allowing alteration of the sail shape. If the deflexer wires are too tight they cause the leading edge tubes forward of the cross tube to be bent inwards. This may produce undesirable fullness in the nose portion of the sail. It will also spread the after ends of the leading edge tubes, making the sail lighter and flatter. No adjustments should be made to the rigging of your rogallo unless you know exactly what the effect will be. In any case, adjustments must be made equally on both sides of the wing. Read the manufacturer's instructions.

2.4. The theoretical glide path of a rogallo in no wind. The real glide path is steeper because the pilot loses height during his take-off run; may not fly accurately at the best speed; flies into almost still air near the ground; and starts his landing flare too high.

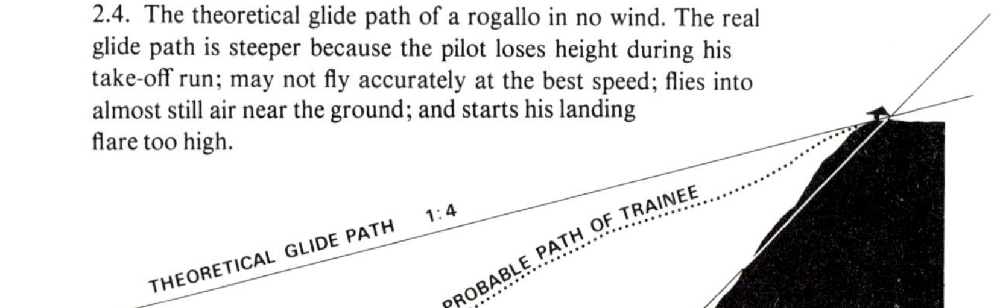

Performance

The performance of any sort of glider is described by its *glide ratio* and by its *sink rate*. The glide ratio, or the ratio of lift to drag which is approximately equivalent, gives the longest distance that the aircraft will travel from a given height. A standard rogallo has a glide ratio of about 1:4 which means that from a 200-ft hilltop it will glide, without needing to soar, a distance of 800 ft. (Fig. 2.4.) A high aspect-ratio sailwing may achieve up to 1:8. Anything that can be done to reduce the drag, from a well-cut sail to a prone harness, or even the elimination of flapping trouser legs, will help improve the glide ratio. The weight of a heavy pilot does not of itself do much to spoil the performance; he will just have to fly faster to achieve the same glide ratio. However, this higher speed will worsen the effect of any drag-producing factors, like a badly stretched sail or those flapping trousers.

Minimum sink is probably a more suitable performance criteria for a slow-speed aircraft, although more difficult to measure. The lowest sink rate of an ordinary rogallo is about 2 m/sec. The flying speed, at which this occurs, however, is usually very close to the stall, and it is usually safer to exchange this lowest possible sink rate for a slightly higher speed with better control over the handling of the aircraft. For minimum sink the heavy pilot is at a disadvantage compared to the lightweight.

Individual hang gliders will be found to fly slightly differently from other apparently identical aircraft. Whether yours flies well or not will depend on the fabric and the way it was cut and has subsequently stretched. It will be affected by rigging wire adjustment, the amount of reflex and the position of the pilot weight in relation to the centre of balance of the wing. Before buying a hang glider it is wise to have a good look at as many as possible and talk to people with a lot of flying experience, and to manufacturers. When you have made your choice obtain all the information and advice that you can so that you will have got everything on the aircraft right—before you get airborne.

CHAPTER THREE

You and hang gliding

Learning to fly properly cannot be achieved in a few days. It is a gradual process, and you need a common-sense attitude to all that you do. Hang gliding is fun but can be ruined so quickly if you become overconfident and fly in conditions that are too much for your experience. On the other hand if you are an underconfident pilot you can have an accident purely through hesitating, or by being pushed into doing something you are not ready for by other pilots or onlookers. You should ask yourself, too, why you want to fly at all. If it is for kicks or a laugh, do something else. Any sort of flying is lethal unless you are prepared to take it seriously and make a real effort to learn to do it properly.

When you watch an experienced pilot soaring you may get the impression that he has to be some sort of super gymnast. (Fig. 3.1.) Not so. Anyone with normal good health, who is prepared for a lot of exercise, and who finds no special problems in co-ordinating the activities of his brain with his hands and feet, can become a good pilot. You should not, however, fly if you have dizzy spells, a hangover, or if you are taking any medication. If in doubt check with your doctor.

Before you start to fly yourself, you should spend at least a day, preferably more, on the hill watching others fly and talking to pilots. Do not be afraid to ask questions, hang glider pilots are a friendly lot. If you offer to carry a rolled-up wing back up the hill once or twice they will be even more friendly and you will have begun to get involved.

Clothing

You will soon learn that flying a hang glider will mean a great deal of exercise climbing up hills, and a lot of standing about in winds

3.1 A good pilot makes flying look easy, and you may think he is some sort of super gymnast.

that quickly feel remarkably cold, interspersed with a few short and exciting flights. So the first essential is to obtain and wear suitable clothing. Starting at the feet you need tough but flexible boots with support for the ankles, and at the top end you must have a good well-fitting helmet. The ideal is one that does not cover your ears so that you can listen easily to the sound of the air past your wing. This is not, however, vital and many pilots wear standard motor-cycle crash helmets. In between boots and helmet you will need warm and comfortable clothes for most of the year, such as jeans, two sweaters, and windproof overalls, or at least a well-made anorak. Several layers are best since walking uphill can be warm work and you may want to peel off a layer or so and then put them back on when you reach the top.

Finally you need tough gloves which will not slip on the control bar, and you should not fly without them.

Food and drink

Time passes quickly out on the hill and mealtimes may come and go without you noticing—until you suddenly feel unexpectedly tired. In cold weather take sandwiches, such as cheese and tomato or meat, and a thermos of hot soup or coffee with milk and sugar, or tea. It is worth, as well, keeping a Mars bar or two, or even a few wrapped sugar lumps in your flying suit pocket to eat if you are cold, or feel in want of quick energy. In summer the need is usually much more for liquid refreshment, so take a bottle of ready-mixed squash, or canned soft drinks. Beware, however, of consuming too much fizz—it does not go so well with flying; and if you want to keep your friends, don't leave your food litter scattered over the hill, take it home.

First aid

People can get hurt in most sports, but hang gliding is somewhat different from activities like football because you are often remote from other people, sometimes with not even a road up to your flying site. So if someone gets injured you may find that you are the only person near by to look after the casualty. At the end of this book there is a section on first aid, but better still you should get some proper training so that you know what to do in an emergency.

Insurance

You should never fly a hang glider without at least third-party insurance, as it can now be very expensive to damage some innocent member of the public. You do not even have to be flying; you could have to pay damages even if your parked wing blew over and hit someone. See Appendix Two for address of British Hang Gliding Association.

By now you are likely either to be on your way to becoming a hang gliding fanatic—or it all seems too much like hard work. If in doubt, forget it for the time being or altogether, but if you think hang gliding is really something you want to do, find the best school or club in your area and pay them a visit.

CHAPTER FOUR

Looking after your hang glider

There is only one way to maintain an aircraft, and that is as good as new. If it is allowed to deteriorate and look tatty, it will perform less well and it will also be less strong. The trouble is that you will not know just how much less strong it has become until something breaks. If this happens in the air, which is after all the most likely place, then you have problems. Maintaining a simple hang glider well is just as important as looking after a big jet. Inspection and maintenance is not just a matter of seeing that all of the aircraft seems to be there and that the fabric has no holes. You should understand exactly what each part of your hang glider is there for, how important it is to the primary structure, and what sort of things can go wrong with it. If the rogallo you are inspecting has not been flown for some time you will need to look at it more carefully, and also somewhat differently, from one that is nearly new and has been flying regularly. Your stored rogallo tubes may have been giving an excellent home to mice as well as providing them with plenty of well-chewed terylene nesting material.

The maintenance that is necessary to care for any aircraft can be divided into day-to-day maintenance, annual overhaul, and repairs.

Day-to-day maintenance

Provided that a proper pre-flight inspection is done each time (Chapter Nine) a hang glider is taken out to fly, and provided that it is de-rigged and transported with cables carefully coiled so that they cannot become kinked and the fabric is stowed so that it cannot chafe, very little day-to-day maintenance is likely to be needed on a well-constructed rogallo. Rigging pins should be slightly greased and the aircraft and fabric should be kept clean and away from substances like battery acid. If you have been flying in wet salty coastal air the whole aircraft should be washed with fresh water and dried before it is put away. That is about all.

Annual overhaul

At least once a year every hang glider owner should take his aircraft out of commission, and carry out a thorough and careful inspection, followed by replacing such parts as seem necessary to last for another *full* year, not just for the next few months. Because good soaring weather occurs throughout the year, it is easy to postpone this essential overhaul, so the only way is to fix a date and stick to it.

Firstly, the entire structure should be taken to pieces, with parts labelled if necessary. Each bit should then be thoroughly inspected inside and out using a powerful torch or inspection light. If certain troubles are known to have occurred on other similar aircraft during the last year, even if not of the same make, look even more carefully to make certain that your hang glider is not the next candidate for failure. Tubes which show any denting or any other than the slightest bending, and bolts which are bent or have any thread damage, should be replaced. All alloy tubing should be checked for signs of corrosion including the presence of grey powdery deposits, pits or cracks. If the deposits and pitting are only minute the tubes should be washed and wiped over with a light oil. If, however, the pitting is at all rough to the finger or there is any cracking or pitting around bolt holes, the whole part should be replaced. Do not forget that corrosion may well be present where it cannot be seen between the tube and any bushing or sleeving. If in doubt, ask. Rigging wires that show signs of deep rust, corrosion, kinking, or fraying just have to be discarded; they are too fundamental for any blind eyes. Run cables through pressed finger-tips wrapped in a handkerchief or an old nylon stocking both ways, and also curve the cable near its ends to make sure that there are no tiny broken ends of individual wires sticking out.

Make a really thorough inspection of the fabric, and even if it seems in good condition, have it checked by the manufacturer or a professional sailmaker if it is more than two or three years old. Synthetic fabrics are subject to ultra-violet deterioration, although superficially they may look all right. Lastly, check over your harness, not only for its condition, but to make sure that it still fits you properly—all that climbing up those hills may have altered your shape. Even if the tether rope looks all right, replace it with new rope of the correct specification. It is not a great expense, and is cheap insurance for your peace of mind.

Finally, when you think that you have finished and the aircraft is ready to go, write a list of the work you have done and what parts you have replaced together with a note of any items that showed excessive wear, date it, sign it and put it in a safe place for next year. Better still, keep a log-book for your aircraft. If your club requires periodic checks on aircraft condition, get these done at the same time.

If you are not prepared to do this work yourself, return your aircraft to the manufacturer for a thorough check.

Repairs

There is always a temptation to go on flying after an exciting landing provided that 'the kite looks all right'. It is a temptation that has to be resisted, the aircraft properly inspected, and if necessary, repairs made before it is flown again. Sod's Law dictates that such problems are most likely to arise in the middle of a competition or just when the wind has become soarable, but this is just one of those things that have to be accepted—your hang glider is an aircraft, not a beat-up surfboard. Although the word repair is used here, with a simple rogallo it is much more likely to be a matter of replacement. The decision has to be made whether or not, for example, a leading edge tube can simply be straightened or whether it is a tube that has already been subjected to straightening therapy, or has a tiny crack, and ought to be replaced. (Fig. 4.1.) There will

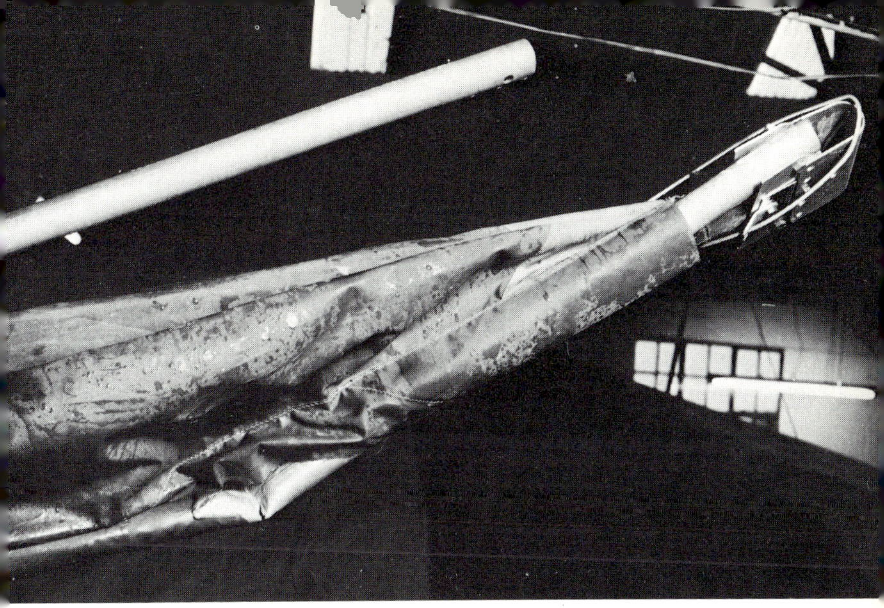

4.1. Broken leading edge tube. The break here is obvious, but a cracked tube which does not tear through the fabric is not. The hang glider should be *thoroughly inspected* after any heavy landing or blow-over.

always be someone around who will tell you that last year they flew their own aircraft with a much bigger crack and it was all right. Let them tell you, but make your own decision or get a competent second opinion, since it is you (and your neck) that is going to fly the hang glider.

Fabric repairs of any size must be patched with identical material and seamed with at least $\frac{1}{2}$-inch hems on both sides. Worn or broken stitching at seam ends or around bolt heads should be restitched before flying again using terylene thread. (Figs. 4.2–4.3.) If a seasick sailor can mend his sails on a gyrating boat, you can do it on a large comfortable hill. As with maintenance, the best policy with repairs is, if in doubt get a second opinion. There is no place in flying for mistakes, and people who have been flying a long time know just how easy it is to make mistakes and they have no hesitation at all in asking for help or advice. But apart from that, a really smart aircraft in beautiful condition will always find admirers—and is a pleasure to fly.

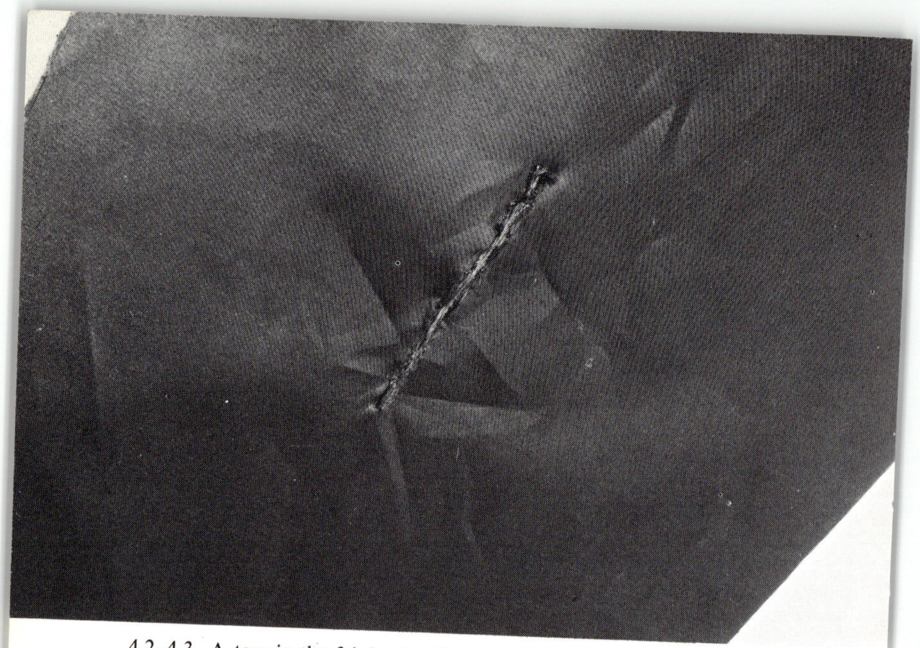

4.2–4.3. A tear in the fabric should first be sewn together neatly (Fig. 4.2) and then be patched using good overlaps and a double row of stitching (Fig. 4.3). The patch in the pictures is of course on the other side of the sail.

5.1. The Gower peninsular at Rhossili in Wales gives smooth lift in westerly winds.

CHAPTER FIVE

Where to fly

The careful study of hills will become a great part of your flying activities. In some areas the choice of hill may be very limited, and there may be a tendency to use the nearest hill on the assumption that the others will be no better. However, quite insignificant details in the shapes of slopes can sometimes make a great deal of difference.

How air behaves over hills is actually remarkably complex, so the best way to find out on a strange hill is to walk over it, feel the direction of the wind on your face and note how and where it changes, and watch the antics of bits of grass you throw into the air. Try to 'see' the wind blowing over and around the hill, in the same way that you see water ripples flowing from a rock in a stream. Look as well at the hill as a whole and its relation to the surrounding countryside, particularly upwind.

The ideal hill rises smoothly from a flat plain or the sea, has a steep face, and rounds out into a large and substantially flat top. (Figs. 5.1 and 5.2a.) It must also have length so that the wind is forced to rise up over the top and not simply curl around the ends. For soaring the gradient should not be less than 45°.

Less suitable hills are those which are hog-backed, rising up one side and descending behind the narrow spine. They are hazardous if you are blown back while trying to land on top. Sharp-edged cliffs are also unsuitable except for the very experienced. They have severe turbulence or dead areas below the crest and just over the crest itself, and in some cases a safe take-off will not be possible. (Figs. 5.2b and c.)

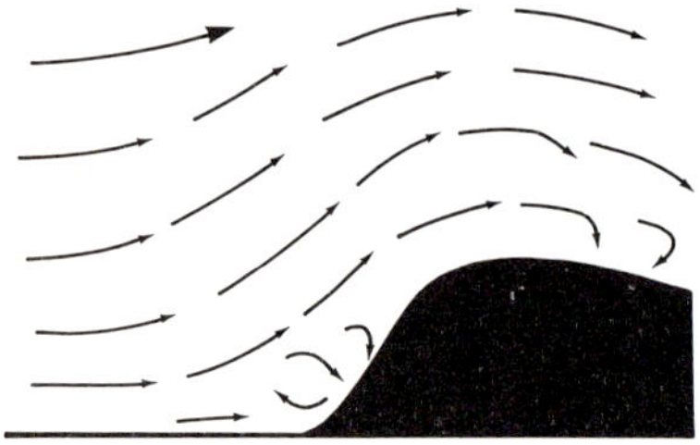

a

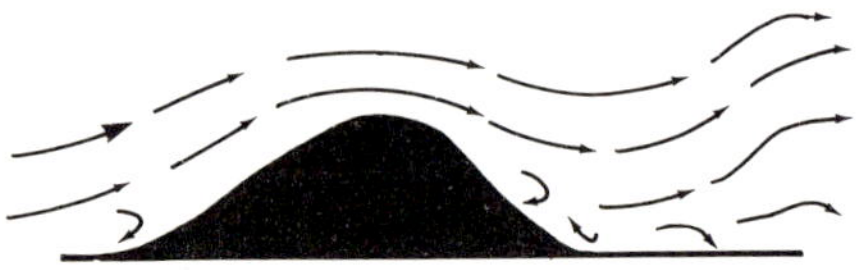

b

c

5.2. a, b, c. Airflow over a smooth rounded hill and over a sharp-edged cliff. The eddies and turbulence may be enough in fresh winds to cause the pilot to lose control.

Bowls or large gulleys can be soared but only if the wind is blowing directly into them. If the wind is sweeping across them they may be found to be surprisingly 'empty' of air. The shape of the bowl or gulley is obviously important, and it may be possible to get trapped in a deep one without room to turn. (Fig. 5.3.) Many ridges have spurs and these will sometimes provide good lift, although they are unpredictable; sometimes it is there and sometimes it is not. Even if the slope itself is of ideal shape and steepness it may be useless for soaring if it is partially blanketed by another ridge close upwind. Use your judgement here. Obviously the further away the other hill the less effect it will have, but it may spoil the lift below a certain height above the ridge. If you can find the lift and keep high you will stay up, but if you allow yourself to descend below the invisible change in the flow pattern you will sink to earth.

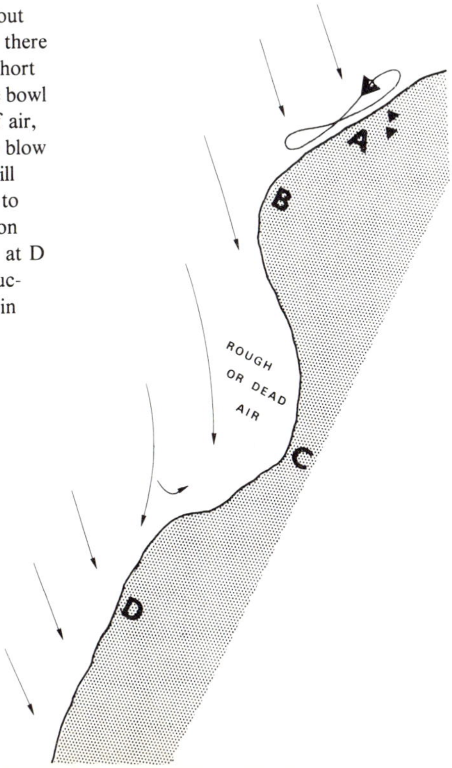

5.3. Walk over a hill to find out what the wind is doing. At A there is likely to be good lift on a short beat. In this wind direction the bowl at C may be almost empty of air, although if the wind swings to blow directly into the bowl there will probably be good lift from B to almost D. In the wind direction shown the lift along the ridge at D may be erratic as the wind fluctuates slightly in direction or in gusts.

5.4. A thermal rising ahead of the hill will flow up the slope and modify the ridge lift by pulling in air from all around.

On a warm summer day thermals forming in the valley will tend to flow up the slope on inland hills. (Fig. 5.4.) Their passage will modify the slope lift by pulling in the wind from all around. If you think you are in thermal lift try heading into wind, S-turning if necessary to keep in the upflow. If you find sudden turbulent sink, you have probably fallen out of the back, or downwind side of the thermal. Any obstructions on the slope, including those some distance out upwind of the foot of the hill, will create turbulence and locally change the wind direction in their vicinity. This will also affect the air for some distance downwind. Trees on the slope are a problem as they disturb the band of lift that hang gliders use.

At any time when soaring close to the ground remember that the wind will be blowing more slowly close to the surface due to the frictional effect of obstructions—the wind gradient. A calm sea and flat beach will create little wind gradient effect, whereas rows of trees, walls or houses produce incredibly powerful gradients. When calculating wind strength remember to check it at the foot of the slope as well as at your take-off point on top to get some idea of the amount and strength of the wind gradient. This will help you to know how much you will have to increase your speed to have a safe margin when coming in to land. (Fig. 5.5.) You can often tell where the gradient will have the greatest effect on your flight by

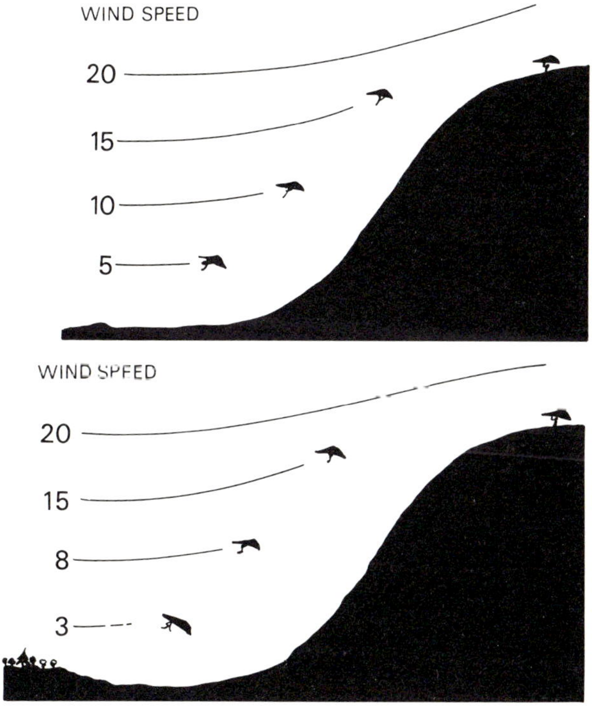

5.5. The speed of the wind lessens near the ground due to surface friction. The gradient is sharper when the surface is broken by buildings, trees, etc, when the wind on the ground may be nil. A hang glider flying at an airspeed of 22 mph will be penetrating at only 2 mph after take off. As it gets lower it will penetrate better, but will also tend to lose airspeed as it descends into the rapidly decreasing wind speed.

walking up or down the face of the slope and feeling the differences in wind strength and direction. A windsock at the bottom of the hill as well as the top will help. Use any aids to wind direction such as ripples in long grass, or smoke.

No matter what hill you decide to fly from the greatest lift will occur when the wind is blowing straight on to its face. Even if it is only 25° off, the lift may be reduced by as much as a third.

CHAPTER SIX

When to fly

Good hang gliding weather occurs all the year round. In fact slope soaring is often better in winter and early spring than it is in summer, because the wind is often stronger and smoother. Training can be carried out in any weather that does not give steady rain or snow, fog, or winds that are too strong. If you fly, understanding the weather and how the air behaves is just as important as knowing how to handle your aircraft. It helps you get more flying by not missing good weather opportunities, and it reduces the frustration of hanging about on a wet and windy hilltop when the weather is unflyable.

Getting to know the weather is partly a matter of understanding, how to interpret weather maps and forecasts, but mainly the direct observation of your own eyes.

Getting a forecast

Forecasts are issued at frequent intervals by radio, TV, newspapers, and by local meteorological offices. These forecasts are intended to cover large areas and so cannot show local modifications to the broad weather pattern. In general forecasts provide a substantial amount of truth, but timing—e.g., when the rain will start—is more likely to be incorrect. This is because the character and speed of movement of the air is constantly altered by very small changes in pressure and temperature hundreds of miles away or many thousands of feet up. This is where you can help yourself. If you know what to look for, and keep looking, you will be able to tell whether that rain is being delayed or is coming in faster than expected.

Maps give a diagrammatic picture of air behaviour (Fig. 6.1), and the quickest way to extract from them the information you want is to

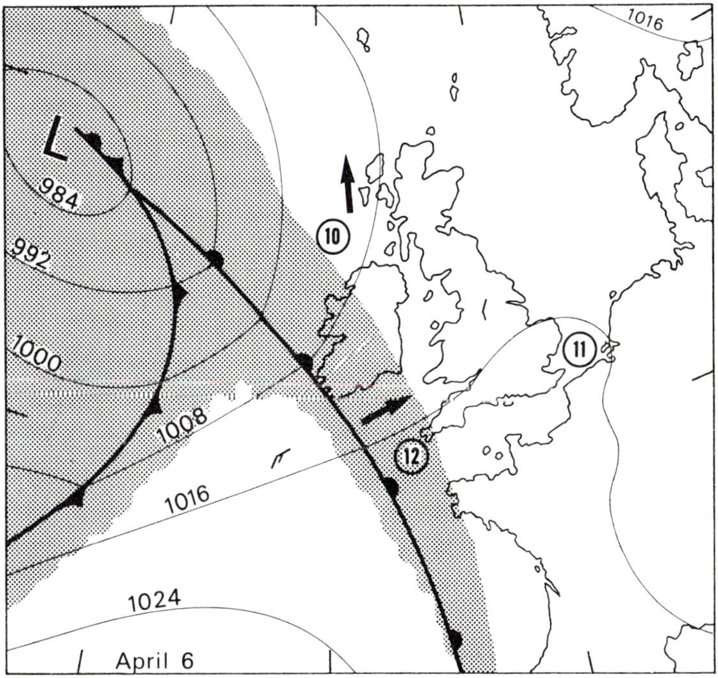

6.1. A Depression or Low. A Low brings generally wet weather with large areas of extensive and thick cloud. In Britain it comes in mainly on SW winds with falling pressure. The warm front, shown by the line marked with half-circles, brings drizzle and hill fog. Following this front the wind will probably veer more westerly with the rain ceasing but the sky remaining cloudy. In an active depression the cold front (spiked line) follows the warm sector with a further veer in wind, and quite often squally showers, heavy rain or even hail. In the day or so after the passing of the cold front there is often good soaring weather with NW winds.

When a depression is old the two fronts may run together, and when even older there may be little or no rain. Temperature in Centigrade is shown in the circles. The wind direction is indicated by arrows with each feather indicating 10 knots and a half-feather 5 knots.

study the newspaper map each morning together with the current forecast, and then observe what happens during the day. If the forecast is wrong try to work out why—did the trough slow down, or the cold front slide away to the north, or the anticyclone collapse and allow a waiting depression to quickly penetrate, or what? After you have done this for a while, try looking at the morning map without using the official interpretation, and make up your own forecast. See how this turns out, and afterwards compare it with the official one.

Although getting a feel for the general weather can save you wasted journeys to a gale-swept hill, this is, of course, only half of what you need to know. The other, and even more important bit is learning to understand the local weather, because this is the air that you are going to fly in. Primarily you want to know what the wind is going to do—whether it will remain substantially steady in strength and direction, or not? Is the wind going to increase, perhaps suddenly, as it does in squalls, or is it likely to change direction, as it probably will with sea-breeze penetration? Or is it going to die away?

The winds

Very generally, and disgracefully oversimplified, winds over Britain have the following characteristics.

N–E: Usually associated with dry weather which may also be hazy. Often hot in summer and cold in winter when there can be an unpleasant raw dampness on the east coast. When strong this anticyclonic wind often contains an odd cobblestone turbulence unlike the surge gustiness of north-westerly air. North-easterly winds tend to remain fairly constant sometimes over quite long periods and they also tend not to die away very much, if at all, in the evenings and at night; remaining strong as long as the high pressure centre remains constant. Near this centre winds are light but tend to strengthen progressively towards the periphery of the anticyclone. When blowing along the coast such winds may often be stronger than indicated in the forecast.

E–S: Winds come least often from this direction, and when they do blow they tend to have much of the character of south-westerlies if they are frontal in origin, or of north-easterlies if they are anticyclonic.

S–W: Winds from this quarter are most often associated with lowering pressure and the increasing cloudiness that goes with it. The air tends to be relatively stable and the winds steady, except that they usually increase as the weather worsens. Because the air is moist from its travels over the Atlantic and because the whole air mass is ascending, cloud forms readily even below hilltop level. On their worst behaviour south-westerlies bring drizzly murk, and on their best, steady and pleasantly mild breezes.

W–N: The direction from which come squalls and April showers, and the rising pressure following the passing of a Low. The air is clean with reasonable or good visibility, and cool or cold in winter and spring. North-westerlies usually freshen up during the day, becoming quite turbulent and gusty, and then die away in the evening. When the wind is strong there may be quite big gust surges from time to time, and turbulence can be severe in squalls.

Obviously, winds cannot be neatly divided into character sectors and there will be overlapping in practice. There are other factors, too, that affect the general behaviour of the wind, such as the terrain. Wind will locally alter speed and direction as it swirls around bluffs or gullies.

Thermals and sea-breezes

The sun produces thermals which, as well as producing lift cause temporary fluctuations in wind strength and direction as they lift off. But the greatest effect of the summer sun for the coastal

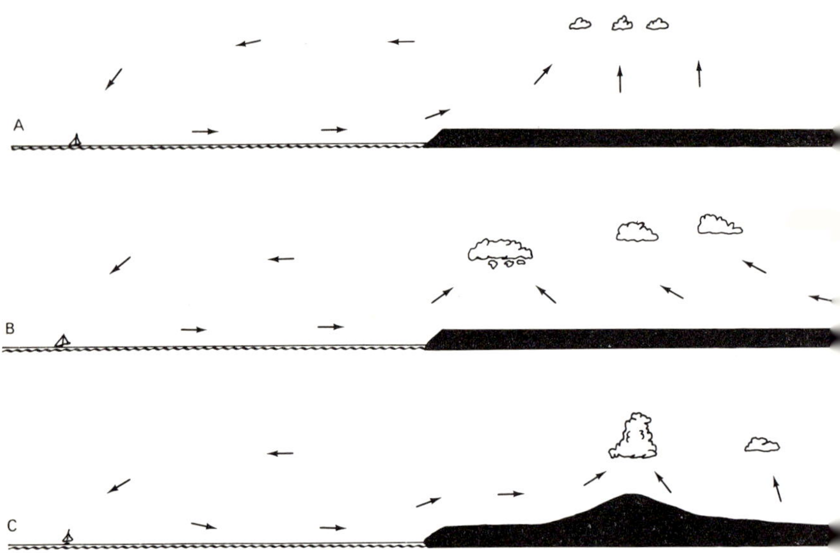

6.2. Sea-breezes. (A) air rising over the land on a warm sunny day is replaced by cooler air pulled in from the sea, (B) when there is a strong opposing prevailing wind from the land a line of cloud may develop where the two winds converge, (C) a line of clouds may also develop over hills a short distance inland.

pilot is to create sea-breezes, which develop in the morning after the sun begins to warm up the land. As warmed air rises inland cooler air is pulled in from the sea to replace it. The rate at which the sea-breeze front moves inland depends on the amount of heating reaching the surface of the land, being low when there is high cloud cover, or when the generally prevailing wind is strong or cold so that the surface is kept cool. The strongest sea-breezes occur when the summer sun climbs high quickly and warms the ground through clear, clean air in a calm or light wind. In the morning the wind at the coast will be the same as everywhere else, for example, light NE. As the land warms up this offshore wind will drop on the coast as the landward pull of the sea-air begins. Then, after a short pause a wind, initially cool, will start to blow from the sea towards the main mass of the land. It will strengthen during the day and gently die away in the late afternoon or early evening. If there is high cloud or extensive flattening out of cumulus so that the overland heating is reduced, any sea-breeze will die away earlier. (Fig. 6.2.)

The transition zone or front between the general wind and the sea-breeze moves steadily inland during the day, perhaps as much as 20–30 miles. If, however, the overland heating is weak it may move inland only as far as the first line of hills or downs. Sometimes there is an unstable convergent flow because the main land-wind and the sea-wind meet at an angle to each other and quite large banks of cumulus clouds may develop along this line with strong lift underneath. This will affect hills near the coast that are used for slope soaring, depending on the location of the line of cloud relative to the hill. If the upflow of the slope lift and the convergence zone coincide the lift will be augmented, but if they are out of phase, as for example, when the line of the convergence zone lies half a mile or so upwind of the soaring slope, the slope lift may be seriously weakened.

Valley-winds

The wind may also behave in an unexpected fashion in valleys, but it is only unexpected to the unobservant, since valley-winds follow an almost boring pattern. Unless the main wind is extremely strong, or coincides with the line of the valley, the local wind will tend to blow up the valley towards higher ground during the day and down towards the valley-floor during the evening and at night. The daily wind up the valley will bias itself to rise leaning against the sunny side of the valley, balancing this with sink over the shady side. Above the valley the wind will return to the main prevailing direction.

Low cloud

One of the temptations when slope soaring in damp, cloudy weather is to continue to fly in worsening weather until cloud—orographic cloud—suddenly starts to form all around, including underneath. This is most likely to happen in the moist SW winds that precede an approaching Low. Since this orographic cloud often develops quickly enough to cut off escape to your landing place, a return to earth should be made the instant any little rags of cloud begin to appear below general cloudbase. When soaring over cliffs any patches of sea-fog drifting about even quite a long way from the land should be watched. They, too, may not only develop rapidly but may be carried in with the sea-breeze to wash around the cliff below you and cut you off from a safe beach landing.

Storms and squalls

Thunderstorms and frontal squalls give very visible and often noisy warnings, but they are quite different in character and behaviour. The summer heat thunderstorm grows usually in the late afternoon, moves fairly slowly accompanied by ominous rumblings, and causes the wind to behave erratically. To a low-performance glider, like a rogallo, flying at no great height, it is not likely to be much of a threat since the air circulation in a heat thunderstorm is such that as it approaches the wind dies, killed by the voracious appetite for air of the storm itself. Everything sinks to earth and the quick-witted will just have time to pack the aircraft away before the storm breaks. (Fig. 6.3.) With gliders of higher performance there is a real risk of getting caught in the powerful updraught in the front part of the storm, and any sign of this happening should set the alarm bells ringing. Without instruments, skill, and a parachute, disaster is almost certain.

Frontal squalls and the wilder April showers move fast. They come whistling in, usually on a fresh-to-strong NW wind, bringing severe gustiness, a much lower cloudbase, and heavy rain, hail or snow. To stay soaring on a hill while such a squall is passing over is Niagara tightrope stuff. They come more quickly than you might expect if they are still growing, as well as moving along in the wind.

6.3. An approaching thunderstorm will firstly bring a period of calm (the calm before the storm) followed by severe gusts blowing out from the storm itself ahead of rain or hail. Gliders should be landed and secured before a squall arrives.

And it is almost impossible to see anything at all if you find yourself flying in snow. Gliders should be landed and secured while it is possible to see enough of the side of the approaching squall cloud for it to still look pretty. Apart from the direct hazards of flying in heavy rain, hail, or snow, the battering on your face and body is a great think killer at a time when clear thought is badly needed.

But even in a country of erratic weather like Britain, it is not necessary when local soaring to get caught out by weather—because you can see it coming. It helps, too, if you are prepared to put a few numbers into your calculations like 'that squall is upwind over Blackberry Hill 8 miles away, now, and the wind is 24–25 mph. I should, therefore, plan to be on the ground in 20 minutes at the latest, say 15 minutes to be safe.'

7.1–7.2. Starting on a two-seater helps the new pilot to become used to the sensation of flying and to overcome his initial natural apprehension.

II LEARNING TO FLY

CHAPTER SEVEN

What it takes to be a pilot

While you are watching others fly, and waiting to get airborne yourself, notice how hang gliders are moved about on the ground and parked. Watch carefully how the pilot takes off and how he is sometimes helped by an assistant. Observe how the landings are made—both the good and bad ones. Above all start to develop a feel for the wind, so that you notice when it becomes gustier, or slackens, or changes direction. Look for such indicators as bonfire smoke in the valley as well as windsock or other pointers on the hilltop. Whenever you walk down the hillface, notice how the wind strength lessens as you get lower.

The best way to learn to fly is to join a school, or a club, so that you can concentrate to begin with on the actual flying, and not have to worry as well about whether the hill or the wind is suitable.

There are several ways that you can learn:

1 On a two-seater with an instructor.

2 Solo, and in radio contact with an instructor.

3 Solo, with care and good advice before every take-off.

These are not, of course, separate systems, and in practice you will probably get some experience of all of them. However, if you have to learn on your own with only advice from a more experienced pilot *you must progress very slowly and with extreme caution*, because there will be no aids to saving you from the consequences of any mistake you may make.

Learning on a two-seater

This is probably the best way to start for many people—even the bravest is trembling on his first take-off. (Figs. 7.1. and 7.2.) It gets you over the first hurdle of realising that you have got your feet off the ground and the only thing supporting you is the wing, and it gives you the necessary respect for your aircraft in the acknowledgement that it is more than capable of supporting you. It is also a great advantage to experience straight away the correct flying speed and attitude and a good landing at first hand, but without the worry of having to try to do all this yourself. A good instructor will talk you through the flight explaining what he is doing, and often requesting your co-operation with certain manoeuvres.

The ideal programme on a two-seater rogallo is an initial air experience flight, followed by a few flights during which you take more of an active part in the control of the aircraft. When your instructor thinks you are capable he will ask you to control the whole flight, while being ready to take over in case of error. Once you have successfully accomplished this you will be ready to progress to a single-seater and be able to fly with the confidence and necessary knowledge of a safe pilot.

However, you still have a long way to go before becoming an experienced pilot and this you can only do on your own, flying solo. It will still help a great deal if you can draw on the assistance of an instructor to explain what you did wrong and to brief you before flying, so that you make as few and as minor mistakes as possible.

The two-seater is also useful for training pilots under sixteen, the legal minimum age for solo flying, and for giving a trial flight to a person who is not sure whether to start learning or not.

Radio

With this method the pilot flies solo from the beginning, but receives instruction in the air via a radio fitted in his helmet or on the control frame. The instructor starts to talk to the student by radio before take-off, reminding about the actions immediately necessary. During the flight he tells him what speed adjustments to make, when to turn, and when to start to flare out for the landing.

The instructor will say less as the pilot progresses until he is doing it all on his own. Further training will be confined to briefing the pilot on new exercises before take-off, and discussing with him what he did well or badly after landing. (Figs. 7.3–7.5.)

Perhaps the best way of learning is to fly on a two-seater until you have a feel for what is happening and what you should be doing, and then do some flights solo with a radio so that although you are taking all the decisions the instructor can help you correct any errors. Even when you have been flying entirely on your own for a while, a radio helmet link with an instructor will be helpful for early soaring flights. No aids to learning should ever be spurned; there are so many new things to find out in flights of, initially, incredibly short duration, so that there is barely time to think. Any help in reducing the work load so that you will not have to concentrate on quite so many things at once should be fully used.

Learning solo

If you are unable to take advantage of two-seater or radio facilities at a school, then it is essential to progress slowly with the help and advice of an experienced pilot. But make sure your chosen mentor really is a pilot who fully understands what he is doing: there are always a small number of people around prepared to tell others what to do without knowing much themselves. When learning on your own it is most important that you never allow yourself to be pressured into flying. If you do not feel happy, don't fly. *Never* go flying alone, even when you are experienced. Accidents are unpredictable, and even though you may only have a sprained ankle, a night out on an exposed hill in winter can be very serious. Apart from your personal survival, searching for missing people is expensive, tedious, and particularly frustrating when it is unnecessary.

HIWAY

Stages of training

Your basic training, by whatever method, or mixture of methods, is all right provided it is divided into logical stages. Progress will initially be more rapid if it is started on a two-seater, but all the exercises in the first stage (Chapter Ten) should also be carried out solo before progressing further. When you have got some solid flying under your belt and when you have become proficient in slope soaring, the time will have come to start developing your skills and improving your precision. You might even become really good. You will have time, in this further flying, to teach yourself to fly with greater accuracy and neatness, and to concentrate on small but important details like keeping your body at its best aerodynamic shape.

Being a pilot is not just flying

As well as just being able to fly a rogallo, to become a real pilot you need to understand the theory—how and why a hang glider wing obtains its lift and why it stalls, or why altering the amount of reflex will make a considerable difference to how the aircraft handles in the air. You also need to know how to rig your hang glider, how to do a proper pre-flight inspection, and if you damage it, whether to repair it yourself or take it to a professional. You should learn about all these things at the same time as you are doing your flying training, so that when you have become skilled enough to soar in slope lift you also thoroughly understand about your hang glider.

Finally, remember. No matter how much experience you have, always be sensible and respect the elements. The air is very attractive but it is even more unforgiving than the sea.

7.3–7.5. It is best to start with a school in a small group of other beginners and learn under the care of an experienced instructor. This school uses radio helmets to guide the pilot in the air.

CHAPTER EIGHT

Ground handling

Before you even consider making your first flight learn how to handle your glider on the ground. You would be surprised how many are damaged even before their maiden flight through ignorance or carelessness. A hang glider is often subjected to greater stresses while on the ground than it will ever encounter in the air, so it is important to know what can happen, why, and how to avoid unnecessary and expensive damage.

Parking

When you are waiting for a flight and your rogallo is parked at the top of the hill you not only want to prevent it being blown over, but you have a real responsibility for protecting spectators, gliders near by, and other property.

Because a wing will produce lift when it reaches a certain angle of attack it is essential to keep the nose low when you do not want it to fly. The obvious measure is to lower the nose to the ground. Providing the hang glider is pointing directly into wind the air pressure on the sail in this attitude will keep it in the same position. If the nose is at all out of wind it is possible for the wing which is more towards the wind to rise, and the glider will be blown over. Whenever your rogallo is fully rigged it should always be parked nose-down and into wind regardless of its position on the hillside. (Fig. 8.1.) In a crowded situation try to leave at least one span between your aircraft and the next one. If you are leaving your rogallo for any length of time assume that the wind will change, and roll up the sail against the keel tube, or if there is a release on the cables from the control frame, free it and pull the nose forward and down so that the wing collapses flat on the ground, and will not easily blow over.

8.1. Always leave your rogallo pointing into wind with the nose down. If the wind is strong roll up the sail against the keel tube.

Back up the hill

There are three good methods of carrying a rogallo up a slope. All have advantages and disadvantages, but it is worth remembering that too many helpers are worse than none—you can always manage on your own, even though it may be harder work. Hang gliding means a lot of walking, so never walk fast enough to get out of breath, maintain a steady rhythm up the hill, changing gear with your step size as necessary. You will fly less safely if you are tired.

Method 1—single man

This is perhaps the most popular way of carrying a rogallo, and it can be used whether the sail is extended or not. (Fig. 8.2.) Decide

8.2. It is easier to roll up your wing to carry it up the hill, particularly if the wind is gusty or the path to the top changes direction.

on the route you are going to take, and if it will change direction on the way up or the wind is strong then keep the sail folded. If the route is virtually straight and the wind light having the sail extended will actually help you. But keep the nose down and into wind. When the aircraft is partially de-rigged it can be carried in any way that is comfortable.

Method 2—single man

This way takes much of the strain out of carrying your rogallo but it does need practice. You 'fly' your glider up the slope, or along it if you wish to move your position at the top. (Figs. 8.3 and 8.4.)

Keeping the nose into wind raise it carefully until the sail is just filled and will carry its weight. Holding the two lower forward wires you can control the angle of the sail to the airflow to suit the wind strength. In light winds you can position yourself well in towards the control frame so the nose will be high. In stronger winds you should stay nearer the nose keeping it fairly low.

Method 3—three men

Although you can reduce the load by sharing it, this method is only suitable in very light winds.

One person is positioned at the rear of the keel tube, another at a wingtip, and the third at the control frame. Lift the glider by the

8.3–8.4. A rogallo can be 'flown' up the slope, or moved along the top of the ridge by holding the nose wires, but great care is needed in gusty winds.

8.5. A rigid aerofoil hang glider with wheels can be pushed and lifted up the hill by two people; a wingtip holder is necessary in fresh winds.

control frame and keep the angle of attack high by holding the centre tube and wingtip low. Again, keeping the nose directly into wind make your way up the slope. (Fig. 8.5.) Even in a very light wind this method will make the climb easy. Make sure that your helpers only lift on strong and supported parts of the rogallo structure.

One important point to remember is that if at any time there will be a cross-wind component, the wingtip facing the wind is the one that should be held. It is then easy to control any rise or drop of that wing. The person on the control frame can also alter the angle of attack as necessary by moving to the forward rigging wires.

Knowing how to handle your hang glider both when stationary and in transit will prevent it, or anything else, getting damaged. The golden rule is to lower the nose immediately whenever you stop, or whenever you feel the situation is not under complete control—and make sure that it is pointing into wind. If you see a rogallo on the ground likely to blow over, whether or not it has a pilot, run and grab whatever bit is pointing into wind, and hold it *down*. This will probably be the nose or if it has already swung out of wind, one wingtip. *Never* hold on to, or hold down, any bit of the *downwind* side of the aircraft; you will only succeed in having it cartwheel or blow over on top of you.

9.1. It is easy to be interrupted or talk to friends when rigging or inspecting your hang glider and then forget to finish what you were doing.

CHAPTER NINE

Safe to fly?

Before a hang glider is ready to fly two things have to be done—by you. It has to be put together, and then checked that you have put it together properly and that everything is in good condition. If you fail to do either carefully, and *every time*, you will sooner or later fly an aircraft that will come apart in the air, or you will fall out of it. Whether you like it or not the price of structural or harness failure is very high.

Perhaps the biggest problem when rigging your hang glider is being interrupted before you have finished. Someone wants a hand to get airborne or a friend turns up that you have not seen for months. (Fig. 9.1.) So you stop work and then it is easy to forget how far you had got or even forget to finish the job at all. Since interruptions will never be eliminated you need to have a system. When you first get your glider it is worth making a pocket checklist, and go on using it until your system is automatic. When you do get interrupted there is a simple rule that you can apply when eventually you get back to your aircraft. You re-check the item you were checking when you left, or if you do not remember which it was, you start again to check everything from the beginning. It is not important that this will take a little more time when you are desperate to get airborne, because you will never enjoy a flight with a nagging worry about the security of some now invisible rigging pin, or that the sail fabric is creeping up one of the tubes and spoiling the lift on that wing. There is another good rule that applies to any pre-flight check, and that is that it is done by the person who is first going to fly the aircraft. This does not necessarily apply in a school, but to everyone who considers that they have become a pilot in their own right. It does not matter how many friends help rig, or how experienced they are, each pilot should take responsibility for the hang glider that he is going to fly.

The aircraft should be fully checked every time that it is put together. If it is not dismantled before the next flight and has not made a bad landing only certain items need to be re-checked before getting airborne. Remember that you are looking for two things; to make sure that you have rigged the aircraft correctly, and to see that everything is undamaged and in good condition.

Rigging

1 Erect the control frame attaching the lower rear wires to the rear end of the keel. (Fig. 9.2.) Stand the wing right way up nose into wind, and on the ground.
2 Check that the cross tube is free to rotate. (Fig. 9.3.)
3 Erect kingpost and brace to both ends of the keel tube.
4 Swing out the cross tube, then pull out one side of the wing and attach the leading edge tube to the cross tube. Repeat for other wing. (Fig. 9.4.)

9.2–9.3. Take off the cover and check that all bracing wires are free and have not become kinked, then stand the hang glider on its control frame pointing into wind, and swing out the cross tube.

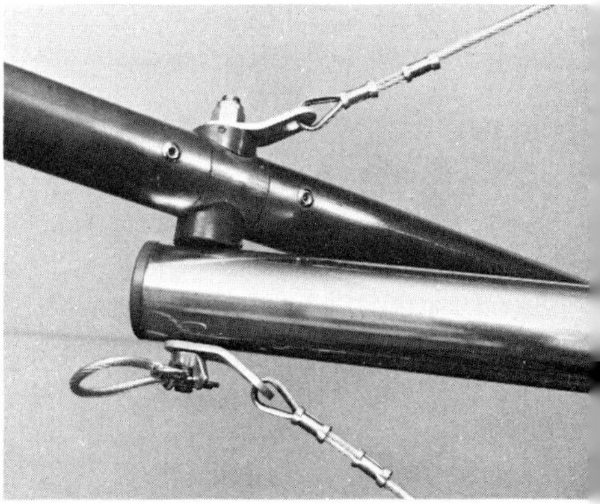

9.4–9.5. Attach and secure the leading edge tube (top) attachment to the keel tube.

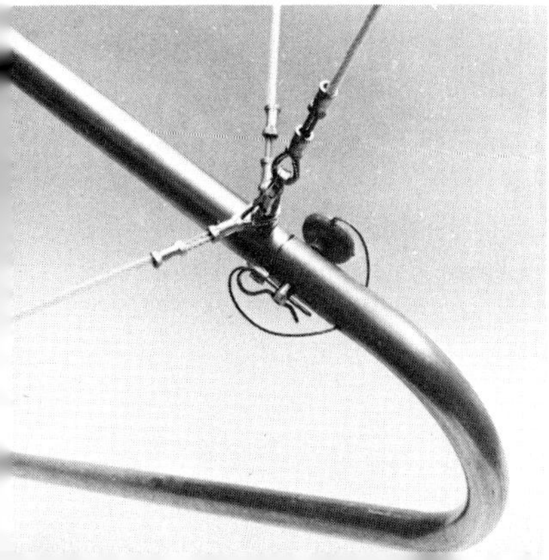

9.6. Bracing wire connection to the control frame. This frame is made in three pieces and is rigged with secured steel pins.

5 Do up bracing wires from kingpost to ends of cross tube, and from control frame to ends of cross tube. If any wire seems tighter than usual check the end fittings are not kinked. (Fig. 9.5.)

6 Raise nose and attach bracing wires from control frame to nose (Fig. 9.6.), and put the nose down on the ground again.

The aircraft is now rigged but it is not ready to fly. It is necessary to see that all nuts are locked, that bracing wires are properly tensioned, that cable ends are not twisted nor the tangs (lugs) bent, and that the correct amount of reflex and dihedral are present.

All these are aspects of rigging, but it is not proposed to go further into details here as each manufacturer produces the correct information for his own product, which should be carefully followed. Read it again.

Pre-flight inspection

First of all stand back and take a critical look at the whole aircraft. Does it look normal and smart, something that makes you feel pleased when you look at it, or does it look slightly distorted or shabby? Is there anything missing, like the harness or your helmet, a safety pin, or is one of the fundamental flying wires lying in the grass? (Figs. 9.7 and 9.8.)

Now go carefully around the aircraft. There are many ways of doing this, and it does not matter which one you use provided that it covers all the essential items. It is logical to start at the nose because you will need to pick this up to inspect it, and you can then put it down again so that the wing will not blow over while you are checking everything else.

1 Nose or apex plate. Check for damage which could have been caused on landing, and that bolts and bracing wire attachments are in good condition and locked. (Figs. 9.9 and 9.10.)

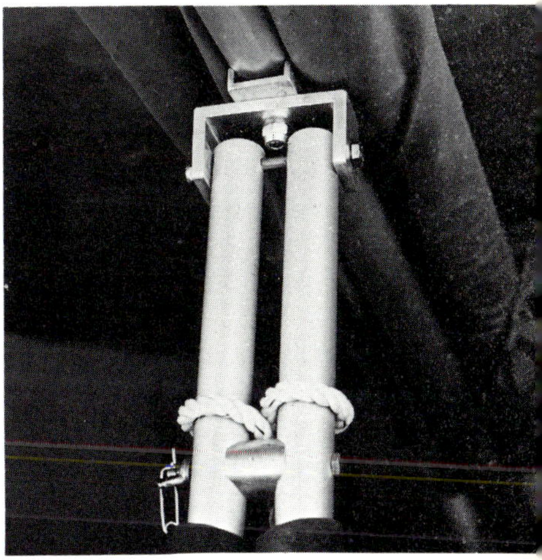

9.7–9.8. Harness attachment at the top of the control frame may be by a steel clip (left) or by a terylene rope link.

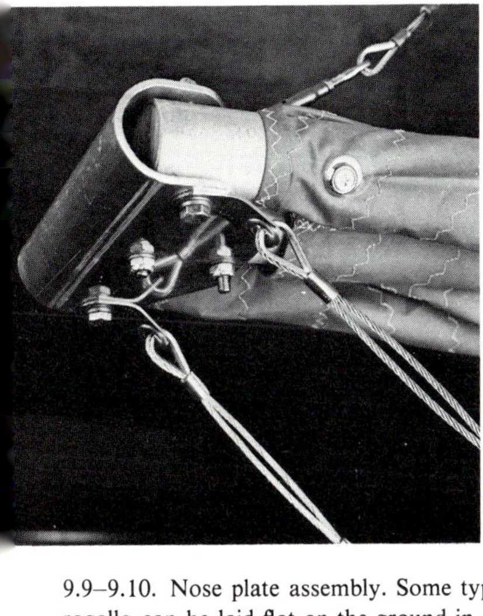

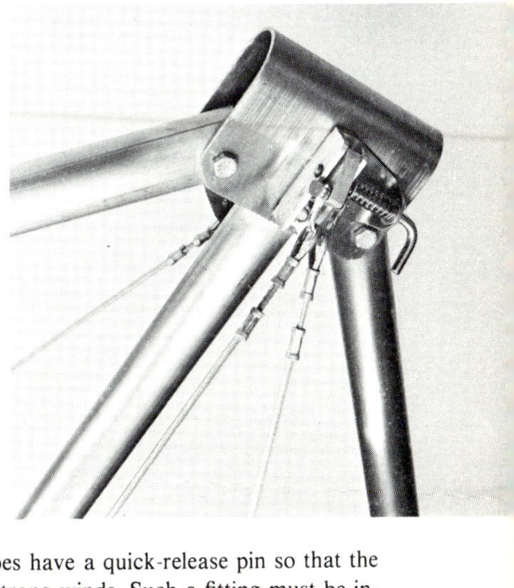

9.9–9.10. Nose plate assembly. Some types have a quick-release pin so that the rogallo can be laid flat on the ground in strong winds. Such a fitting must be inspected before every take-off, in case it has become disconnected.

2 Look down the two leading edge tubes and the keel tube, and check for straightness and reflex.
3 Walk along the leading edge tube checking fabric for tears or worn seams. Check the leading edge/cross tube connection for correct attachment and security. Check that the bracing wires from the control frame and from the kingpost are correctly assembled and locked.
4 Walk along the trailing edge, checking fabric for tears and worn hem. At the rear of the keel tube check bracing wire attachment from the control frame. Check that the amount of reflex is correct. (Appendix Four.)
5 Walk along the further leading edge tube, repeating the checks for the other side, until you are back at the nose.
6 Go to the heart bolt, where the keel tube and cross tube join and check for attachment and security, for any bending of the tubes, and for any tiny cracks in the region of the bolt holes. Do not skimp this, it is not called the heart bolt for nothing.
7 Check that the control frame is properly attached to the cross tube.
8 Check the control frame carefully, including the rigging pins at the lower corners, the tether arrangements and the harness itself. If the harness is on you, do not forget to check it carefully.
9 Finally, look over the sail generally. See that it is not pinched around fittings and that it has no holes. Very *small* holes can be *temporarily* repaired with fablon or pvc tape. See that the trailing edge of the sail is secured on all three tubes. See that any battens are fitted correctly.

If wing wires (deflexers) are fitted (Fig. 9.11), the sail must be checked to ensure that the fabric is correctly tensioned. This is done by inflating the sail and then slowly reducing the angle of attack. Deflation of a standard rogallo sail should start at the trailing edge and work forward. A sail which collapses first at or near the nose while the trailing edge is still inflated and taut is dangerous. It will be prone to luffing.

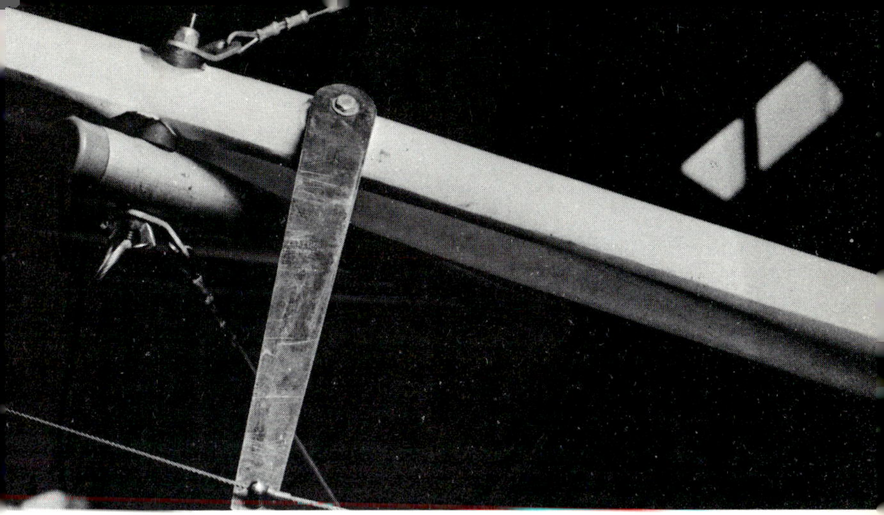

9.11. Wing wire, or deflexer, bracing keeps the leading edge tube from bending under flight loads, particularly when flying fast. Hang gliders without deflexers should have stiffened tubes.

If you have had a heavy landing check the nose plate, tubes for straightness, heart bolt fitting for cracks, cable ends for bent tangs, and fabric for tears. Look at your harness webbing for cuts from sharp stones.

The checklist is not very long, and it does not take much time, but it has to be done properly. This means that you must know what you are looking for, and be suspicious of anything that does not seem quite right. Keep a general look-out for any of the following, at *any* time:

1 A single flying wire that becomes slack during the day's flying.
2 Bolts and pins that have been put in incorrectly with their heads at the bottom, so that if the nut comes off the bolt may fall out as well.
3 Corrosion or tiny whiskers near the ends of flying wires.
4 Turnbuckles (bottlescrews) that do not have at least six turns of thread in the barrel, with the two ends inserted approximately an equal amount.
5 A sail that seems to have become noisier than it used to be. It may be badly stretched or beginning to go at a seam, or along the trailing edge hem.

6 Tether line that has become flattened or which on opening the lay of the rope shows signs of being heat-welded together. It is much weaker.

If all is well, you and your hang glider should now be ready to fly. Unfortunately it does sometimes happen that the aircraft is found to be unserviceable. If it is, and you are the only person who will fly the aircraft, the fact that it is unsafe to fly is important only to you—and you know. If, however, there is any chance that any other pilot may fly it while you are away looking for the necessary bits to do a repair, you must make it obvious that the aircraft should not be flown. Tie a note to the control frame, or take any other action which will ensure that it is not flown in your absence. It is a *law* of the air to report any defect or incident which might affect the safety of other pilots, just as it is a law of the sea to respond to a distress call, however inconvenient.

If your hang glider is handling in a slightly odd way that you do not understand, or you think that you may have done some landing damage even though you cannot find anything wrong, get advice. Tell the person in charge of flying or your instructor, or any person who knows more about hang gliders than you do, so that a double check can be made. If the problem cannot easily be rectified inform the manufacturer. Never let it get deep into your system that you know best—not when flying, anyway.

CHAPTER TEN

First flights

Now at last you can get down to the serious business of flying. It is sensible to think of your future progress in stages, and make up your mind not to progress to a further stage until you have thoroughly mastered the earlier requirements. Even when you feel confident about your flying never forget that quite a small change in wind direction, or an increase in windspeed, can turn flying conditions on a site you are used to into a tricky problem perhaps well beyond your skill.

Stage 1

Assessment of flying conditions. Is the hill suitable for first flights, is the landing area suitable and clear of obstructions, is the weather all right with a smooth wind of not more than 10 mph? If these conditions are right you can start to slowly work your way through:

Take-off, flying straight, and landing.

Control over your airspeed.

45° turns.

S-turns with the landing into wind.

Stage 2

Assessment of flying conditions. The wind can now be a little stronger but it still must not be gusty.

Accurate speed control.

90° turns.

Landing in a predetermined position and into wind.

Stage 3

Assessment of flying conditions. Fresher winds are now acceptable with some gusts, but big surging gusts must be avoided particularly if the wind is not directly on to the hillface.

180° turns.

Flying with other aircraft.

Contour flying.

Soaring.

Stage 4

Further flying, including making the most of the lift, the further effects of control in a turn, 360° turns.

Flying different types of hang glider, and using a prone harness. The next chapters will cover all these subjects but for ease of reference they may not be exactly in the same order as above.

Assessment of flying conditions

The success or failure of your first flights is determined to a large extent by the slope of the hill and the wind strength. The slope should be about 1:3 or 1:2. Less than this and you will have difficulty leaving the ground; more, and the take-off run will be virtually impossible.

The wind should be 10 mph or less; 7–8 mph is ideal and it should not be gusty. Lighter winds create a problem in balancing your wing and give you a longer, harder, take-off run. Stronger winds demand more expertise in handling the rogallo, although take-off will be easier. The wind must not be gusting and it must be blowing directly up the slope. Attempting to fly in a cross wind at this stage is dangerous.

Check the whole slope for obstructions, such as bushes, fences, trees, power or telegraph cables, livestock, and people. The landing area should be reasonably flat and free from ditches and boggy areas.

Take-off, flying straight, and landing

Rig your glider and do your pre-flight check (pp. 60, 62). Now carry it to your chosen take-off position, which should be about 50 ft up the slope. Decide on your landing area—in front of you—and directly into wind. Check again that there are no obstructions, particularly people, further down your slope. Secure your harness attachment. Pull on the top of the control frame until the wing is horizontal, then lower one hand to the cross bar and put the other on one of the uprights so as to give you roll and pitch control while on the ground, or hold both sides of the control frame, whichever seems comfortable and natural for you. (Figs. 10.1 and 10.2.) Lift the wing up, still keeping it at a low angle of attack.

For your early starts it is best to have a helper to ensure that the wing is level laterally, is directly into wind, and is at the correct angle of attack. The two of you share the job of getting everything right so that you will have the best possible control when you take off.

10.1–10.2. Taking off. The hands should be placed comfortably and firmly to exert maximum control.

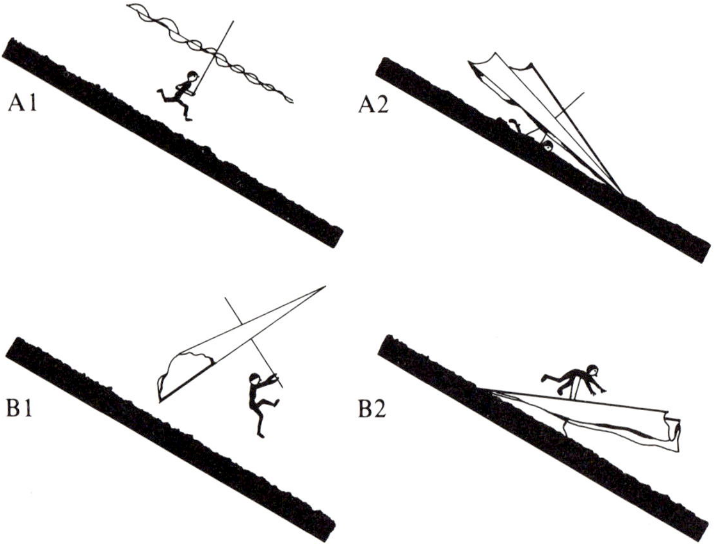

10.3 (A1 & A2) Don't run without pushing out . . . (B1 & B2) Don't push out without running.

Making sure that the nose is directly into wind, increase the angle of attack slightly so that the sail is just beginning to fill and your harness ropes go taut. Most failed take-offs are due to slack ropes. Without hesitating make a determined run and at the same time increase the angle of attack. This is best achieved by pivoting the control frame around a point near its top. Just to push yourself back away from the control frame is not enough. (Fig. 10.3.) Almost immediately you will be airborne, and as soon as you are aware of this pull yourself smoothly towards the control frame to regain flying speed. This is necessary because as soon as you are airborne you will be gliding down a flight path of 1:4 or at best 1:5 and the angle of attack has to be related to the flight path, and not to the horizontal.

When you are flying at the correct speed and attitude concentrate on keeping it like that. Think of your body as part of the aircraft. If the speed starts to drop off pull yourself towards the con-

10.4–10.5. The landing should be made directly into wind towards a clear and unobstructed area. As the ground approaches the pilot pushes his weight back to slow the hang glider and land on his feet.

trol frame slightly, and if speed increases push away. Notice the noise the wing makes when you are flying at the correct attitude. It will go quiet when you are flying more slowly, and become noisier as you go faster.

Try to keep facing your chosen landing place. If one wing drops push yourself away from it transferring weight to the opposite side, until the wing becomes level again. When you are about 10 ft above the ground start to push yourself gradually away from the control frame and keep on pushing until you land—*on your feet.* (Figs. 10.4 and 10.5.) It will help to throw your legs backwards to get yourself really vertical. As you touch down your arms should be fully extended, your groundspeed almost zero, but you should not be sinking rapidly. When trying to guess your height above ground to start your landing flare try to gauge your approximate 10 ft while you are looking ahead. Do not try to guess your height by looking down—you won't be able to judge the landing flare properly.

Immediately you are on the ground drop the nose of your glider. Your flight has not finished until you have done this. You can then release yourself from the hang glider and relax.

Obviously, it will take a number of flights to accomplish all this neatly. Because your take-off point is at no great height you will have to make your control adjustments in quick succession; but try to keep movements as smooth as possible.

Once you have taught yourself to take off cleanly, can fly straight, and land on your feet every time, you are ready to move up the slope. You will now have a little more time in the air, but this will also make you more susceptible to direction changes, wing dropping, and speed loss or gain. Be prepared for this and be ready to make the necessary corrections. After some satisfactory short flights your progress up the slope will become more rapid, but do not get overconfident and miss a few stages by going straight to the top. With height come further complications such as increased windspeed, gusts, and often changes in wind direction. You must always make gradual steps and become competent at each before progressing.

Control over your airspeed

You must teach yourself to be aware of your speed *always*. With experience you will be able to tell when you are going at the correct speed by listening to the noise of the wing, feeling the airflow on your face and seeing the attitude at which you are flying. You will also become accustomed to the position of the control frame in normal flight. This is known as the neutral position (Fig. 10.6) and should be such that your arms are bent, so that you will be able to

10.6. Practice is needed to fly accurately at the right speed, and is helped by the pilot being comfortably in the neutral position.

obtain about equal movement both forwards and backwards in relation to the control frame. Do not spend time looking up at the nose. Try to keep your outlook roughly aligned a little below the horizon. This will enable you not only to see properly where you are going, but your peripheral vision will take in the nose, wingtip, and ground. As you progress up the slope you will find the wind increasing in strength as you get higher. This effect is called the *wind gradient* and it is present even on days of quite light wind.

Wind gradient occurs because the wind near the surface is slowed down by obstructions, such as hedges and trees, to the smooth flow of air. As you fly down through the gradient into the slackening wind you will find that your speed will tend to drop off. If you were to make no corrective movement by pulling yourself in towards the control frame—your loss of speed would mean that you would not have enough control left to flare out and land. Instead you would drop, partially stalled, heavily on to the ground. It is essential to remember to slightly increase your speed at around 50 ft so that when you start to push away at about 10 ft you will have enough control to make a really positive increase in the angle of attack; particularly if there is any wind gradient.

When you are taking off from higher than 150 ft and confidently controlling your flights try this exercise in speed control.

Once airborne and at the correct flying speed, and comfortably in your neutral position, pull yourself forward on the control frame and gradually increase your speed. Notice the feel and sound of the air and the pull of the control frame. Your sail may also begin to flutter slightly at the trailing edge. Remember that your rate of descent will increase as you fly faster, so be ready for this and ease off excess speed before flaring out to land. It is not, of course, necessary to dive at all steeply when doing this exercise. Now do another flight and this time reduce speed slightly; notice the differences in feel, sound, and rate of descent. Make sure, this time, that you have regained sufficient speed before starting the landing.

As you do more flying and get the feel of your rogallo better, go on trying to improve your speed control so that you can fly really accurately. Apart from enabling you to soar better it will help you avoid an accident in a difficult situation.

CHAPTER ELEVEN

Turns

45° turns

The time has now come to attempt your first turn. You can do stand-up landings every time, you can land along a line that you chose before take-off, and you can control your speed accurately.

Before take-off choose your landing line as usual, but also choose a landmark in the distance approximately 45° off this line. (Fig. 11.1.) Once in the air and flying at the correct speed move yourself to the side on which your landmark is situated. The wing will bank and the nose will begin to swing round in the same direction. As it approaches your landmark move yourself back again

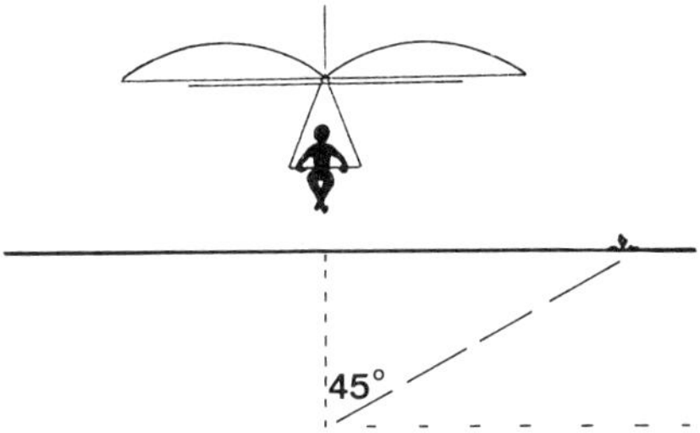

11.1. First turns should be practised by selecting some landmark about 45° to the straight line of flight, turning gently towards it and then stopping the turn as the landmark comes ahead. A gentle turn back into wind should be made before landing.

past neutral and on to the opposite side until the nose is pointing into the wind once more. Re-position yourself at neutral. Continue the flight straight ahead with the wings level.

As with all new manoeuvres, practise until you can carry them out confidently and neatly. Choose landmarks both to the left and to the right, and make each flight include one 45° turn. End with a stand-up landing facing into wind. Do not attempt your first turns unless your landing area is wide enough to allow into-wind landings offset from your original landing line.

S-turns with the landing into wind

The obvious step from one 45° turn is to straighten up and then immediately do another one in the opposite direction. Make sure you will have enough height to complete the two turns and land into wind. If you find that you are descending faster than you expected, forget the second turn, and get into wind with your wings level before landing.

Pick your two landmarks, one 45° to the left and one 45° to the right. Start your flight as normal, doing the first turn as you have been practising, but as you reach your landmark start a turn in the opposite direction towards your second landmark. Then return to your landing direction directly into wind.

Your flights are now becoming more interesting and more challenging. You must remember, though, that there is a lot still to learn, so exercise all the common sense you have got, and be cautious. Be content to perfect the above manoeuvres and techniques, as they will provide you with a sound basis on which to develop your future flying.

90° turns

By now you will be thoroughly used to taking off from considerable heights and making a controlled flight down to a perfect landing. You will be thinking of soaring and doing your first hour-long flight; and you are one step nearer because you are capable of flying in slightly stronger winds. Once you have mastered all of the following exercises you will be well on the way to being termed a pilot.

Flying conditions

As before, the slope should be free from all obstructions and have a fairly flat landing area. The slope should be about 1:2 or steeper, but not sheer like a cliff—they are for experts only, and even some experts do not like them very much. (Fig. 11.2.) You can increase your windspeed to 15 mph but it must still be steady and blowing directly up the hill. The wind gradient is likely to be more pronounced so check this before flying, and plan your flight so that you will not be left with insufficient speed to make a good landing.

11.2. Soaring on a sharp-edged cliff is for experts only. In front of and just above the top of the cliff the air will be very rough.

11.3. A properly banked turn flown at the right speed. Notice the smooth sail and the almost central position of the pilot now that he is steadily in the turn.

Accurate speed control

Before you progress to 90° turns practise increasing your speed slightly before doing the usual 45° turn. The stalling speed goes up as the turn becomes steeper, so although it was not necessary to increase speed for your gentle 45° turns, it is for steeper turns of 90° or more. If you fly too slowly in a turn the inner wing, which is flying more slowly than the outer one, will stall more fully and the aircraft will slip towards the lower wing at a high rate of sink. (Fig. 11.3.)

Making the turn

Take off from 200–300 ft up the slope and fly straight out until you are past the base of the hill. Remember to increase speed slightly and then make a turn in the usual way, but let it progress until you are facing a point at right angles to your take-off direction. You will now be flying parallel to the ridge, and you will notice how the wind is carrying you back towards the slope. Before you are too close make another 90° turn back into wind, and fly down to land.

11.4. Practice in landing accurately at a predetermined place is always valuable, and competitions soon show up the pilot's skill—or lack of it. The pilot should land on his feet, *not* his bottom.

11.5. A good pilot can stay prone until ready to flare for the landing, assuming the vertical position as he does so.

On your later flights turn through 90° and then adjust your heading so that you are making good a track parallel to the hillface. Then turn out into wind as before. On some flights, make your initial 90° if the site is suitable to the left, and on others to the right.

Notice how the rate of descent increases in the turn. If other aircraft are flying look out for them and avoid taking off at the same time as someone else.

Landing in a predetermined position and into wind

It is essential to be able to land your hang glider where you want to, and not just where it happens to arrive, as sooner or later you will have to make an emergency landing in a hurriedly chosen area. (Figs. 11.4 and 11.5.)

A rogallo travels forward in no wind about four times its height above the ground; from a 100 m (300 ft) hill it will theoretically travel some 400 yds. If anything is obstructing this path which cannot be flown around, it will be necessary to lose height more rapidly. There are three ways of increasing your rate of descent:

1 By increasing speed; this increases the drag.
2 By making a series of turns; this uses up distance.
3 By flying near the stall; this increases the sink rate.

Increasing speed and diving towards your landing area can only be used when you see the situation in good time, as it would take a dangerously steep dive to get you down quickly in a short distance. You are also then left with excess speed which has to be dissipated, usually resulting in a long float before landing.

Turns are the most sensible method of losing height. Make a series of left and right turns out from the hill until you are down to the desired height. But plan them carefully so that you leave enough height in the last turn to be able to face into wind for the landing. Near the top of the hill the wind will prevent you making much headway but as you descend into the lower windspeeds near the foot of the hill you can expect to progress further over the ground.

Flying close to the stall is used effectively by experienced pilots, but it can be very dangerous to a novice. This method can only be used on rogallos which behave like a parachute when flown very slowly. The risks in this manoeuvre are being unable to check the high rate of descent before striking the ground, and that lateral control becomes much less effective.

You can practise position landings by choosing a point along your landing line and controlling your flight path so that you land on it. Gradually bring the target nearer the base of the hill and 45° off track, so that you have to do some very precise flying in order to get there. Wherever you position your target, take off in the normal way and then assess the rate of descent, your groundspeed, and your direction. By making any necessary turns and by precisely regulating your speed endeavour to make a bull's-eye landing. Notice the increased rate of descent when combining a turn with even a quite shallow dive.

Landing up a slope

When landing on an upslope extra speed is needed in order that the hang glider can be flared through the greater angle necessary to make a normal landing. (Fig. 11.6.) Without enough reserve of

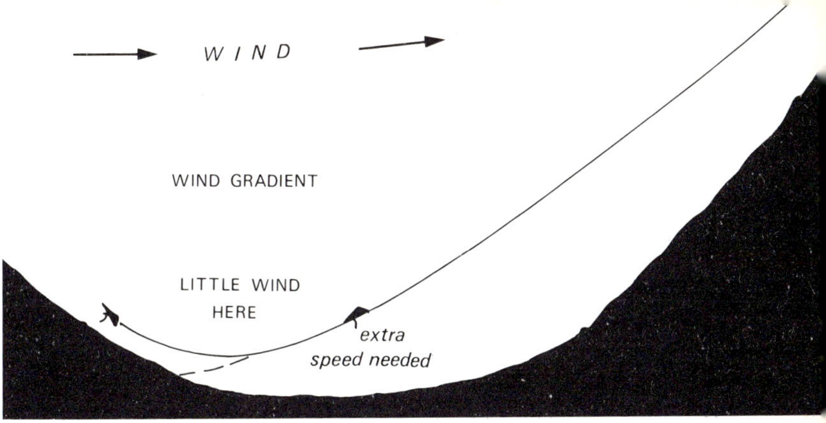

11.6. When landing on an up-slope extra speed is needed to flare through the greater angle necessary. There is often little wind in hollows so without a good margin of speed a heavy landing into the slope will be inevitable.

speed a heavy landing into the slope will result. There is often appreciably less wind in hollows giving a marked wind gradient effect, which is a further reason for having a good margin of speed.

With time you will be able to land both accurately and neatly, and when you can regularly do this within a 50 ft (16 m) diameter circle you will be ready to progress to 180° turns.

180° turns

You are now on the verge of soaring, considered by many to be the mark of an experienced flier. You are certainly no longer a novice but keep an open mind; every flight will teach you something new, and as long as you are sensible it will not be the hard way. It is very important to make your assessment of the site and weather conditions accurately. Convincing yourself that the wind is not too strong when it is, or that the slope is steep enough when it isn't, is just as bad as making no assessment at all. Because you may now be flying in fairly strong winds which will inevitably contain gusts, you must really be aware of what is happening all around you.

Do not start on Stage 3 unless all your control movements are instinctive, as there will not be time to think about which way you should move in order to do a right turn!

Flying conditions

The ridge should have a slope of 1:2 or steeper, and be free of obstructions such as trees, wires, etc. Still check for minor obstructions and bear them in mind, although now you should be able to avoid them. The wind should be between 15–20 mph, and may be up to 30° off the slope. Gusts should not be more than 5 mph in any 10 seconds. Your take-off height should be 300 ft or more. In these conditions soaring will be possible, so don't get swept up by mistake.

Take-off

In such stronger winds it will be necessary to obtain the assistance of an experienced pilot. When you are strapped into your harness and ready to launch ask him to gradually raise the nose until the rogallo is horizontal with the sail flapping. (Figs. 11.7–11.9.)

Keeping the nose into wind raise the wing by the control frame, still keeping the angle of attack low. Your assistant should now be holding the forward wires while you balance the wing laterally and

11.7–11.9. In stronger winds an assistant is needed to hold the nose wires until the instant of take-off. He should help keep the hang glider pointing directly into wind with the wings level. The nose should be held low (Fig. 11.8) with the sail providing no lift.

allow the angle of attack to increase slightly. When you are ready, give the command to release and at the same time run forward. You will immediately be airborne. This method of take-off eliminates the risk of groundlooping which could easily happen in strong winds.

Making the turn

As soon as you are in the air you will notice the lift, but resist the temptation to soar; fly on through it until you are past the base of the ridge. Make a turn and track along the ridge parallel to the slope. Remembering to increase your speed slightly make another turn out from the hill, continuing round for nearly 180° until you are flying back along your previous track. Do one more 90° turn to position yourself into wind for landing. As you descend into the lower wind levels make sure you still have enough flying speed.

Repeat this exercise several times before starting to use the lift for soaring, particularly if you are going to have to share it with several other pilots.

(Fig. 11.9) The nose is raised increasing the angle of attack and filling the sail ready for take-off.

III ADVANCED FLYING

CHAPTER TWELVE

Flying with other aircraft

While you were learning there may have been only a few beginners on the slopes with you who were quite happy to take turns, so you had the air to yourself. Now that you are ready to soar it will be rare on a good day not to have to face the prospect of sharing the lift with at least one other pilot. As with anything else there have to be rules which everybody knows and observes, otherwise collision would be inevitable. Common sense is a valuable asset and manners can help a great deal as well—don't hog the best lift and let everyone else struggle! Before you take off ask your assistant to look all around and let you know when it is clear to go. (Fig. 12.1.)

12.1. Before take-off ask your assistant to look all around and check that it is clear to go.

12.2. (*opposite*) (A) To avoid collision with a hill always turn *out* from slope. (B) If overtaking another glider keep clear and pass between it and hill, so it can turn out at any time. (C) When meeting head-on pass by moving to right.

The rules of the air

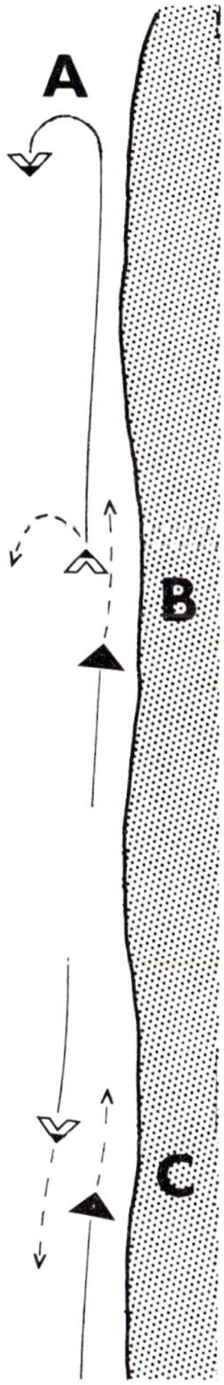

Two aircraft meeting head on: There is a simple rule for this and everyone observes it. Each pilot breaks *right.* (C).

Overtaking: Obviously when several gliders are flying together they are not all at the same point on the ridge at the same time or flying at the same speed. It is inevitable, therefore, that you are going to have to overtake sooner or later. If you decide to pass to windward of another pilot the chances are that he will not have seen you and will turn just as you are passing. Since no one turns in towards the hill when soaring the safe course is to overtake between the other glider and the hill. It is the responsibility of the overtaking glider to keep clear. (Fig. 12.2, A & B).

Converging: This can be dangerous and is often caused by an over-crowded ridge or lack of forethought on the part of one or both of the pilots. Should you find yourself in such a situation, whether it is your fault or not, the pilot nearest the ridge has right of way. If you are to windward, turn out from the hill, even if it means you will go to the bottom.

Landing: Always give way to a lower pilot. Apart from the fact that he has less room to manoeuvre than you he will not be able to see you, and may not even know that you are there. Never fly deliberately in the blind spot of another aircraft. Always keep saying 'Can he see me?'

In marginal conditions several pilots may be struggling to stay airborne, and this is when hazardous situations can arise. Everyone is hugging the hillside to stay in the narrow band of lift and a fiercely competitive spirit may develop.

12.3. A pilot will fly less accurately if he knows there is another aircraft behind him and he cannot see it.

12.4. Keep a good look-out at all times: 'Has he seen me?'

If you are tracking along the ridge to a better area of lift marked by a couple of other gliders, and you reach it with roughly the same height, take care not to box in the centre aircraft. If you do put him in a difficult situation so that he cannot escape by flying out of the lift, you may force him into the hillside.

Whatever the situation try to stay as visible to other gliders as possible. Just because you are higher do not sit above another glider. Its pilot may have seen you arrive and now be worried about where you are; his flying accuracy could suffer as a result. (Figs. 12.3–12.4.) Some schools attach an orange streamer to the kingpost of hang gliders flown by inexperienced pilots.

Hang gliders, like other aircraft, produce considerable wake turbulence, so do not fly too close behind another pilot. If you do have to go through wake turbulence fly through the other glider's track as quickly as possible. If you do have to take evasive action, make sure you do not avoid one aircraft only to run into another. Keep a good look-out at all times, and once again say 'Has he seen me?'

CHAPTER THIRTEEN

Soaring

A glider will soar when it is flying in air that is rising faster than the glider is sinking down through it. If you need an analogy try running down an upgoing escalator. If the escalator is going up faster than you are going down, you will stay up. If, however, the escalator is a feeble one and you descend more rapidly than the escalator is going up, you will eventually arrive at the bottom.

The wind flowing up the hill waiting to support you and your rogallo does not rise everywhere with uniform strength. The good soaring pilot is the one who manages to search out the best bits of lift and manoeuvre to stay in them long enough to gain the maximum height.

Now that you are proficient at 180° turns, accurately controlling your speed, flying in stronger winds and with other pilots, and really understand how to assess flying conditions you are ready for your first soaring flight. This will require all your ability and knowledge. Once again, it is useless attempting this stage if you are still having to think about control movements, they must definitely come naturally.

If it is at all possible choose a site or a time when there are few other fliers. The less you have to worry about the more you can concentrate on what you are doing.

The minimum wind necessary to soar easily is 15 mph, and *smooth.* Take off in the usual manner, remembering to ask an experienced pilot to hold the forward wires for a safe controlled start. As your feet leave the ground you will be aware of a buoyant feeling rather than the usual sinking one. (Fig. 13.1.) This is lift! As you gain height check that you are flying at the right speed, and you are not moving backwards into the hill. If you are, increase speed slightly more. (Fig. 13.2.)

What you are now trying to do is to stay in the rising band of air above and in front of the ridge. It will be roughly half the height of

13.1. The hang glider immediately feels buoyant when it takes off into lift.

13.2. If the wind is as strong as, or greater than, the flying speed of the glider, the pilot may find himself travelling backwards over the hill.

the hill in width. To stay in this lift you will have to beat back and forth along the ridge making a series of 180° turns at each end of the slope—always outwards away from the hill. Start by making a turn of something less than 90° along the slope adjusting your track so that it is parallel to the ridge and a little upwind of the crest. (Fig. 13.3) You will not be pointing in the direction that you are flying over the ground, but crabbing along. (Fig. 13.4.) The stronger the wind the less you will need to turn in order to produce the parallel track. If the wind strength were equal to your flying speed, you would not need to turn at all. You would just remain poised in the lift, stationary over the ground. But you should not be flying in winds as strong as this for a long time.

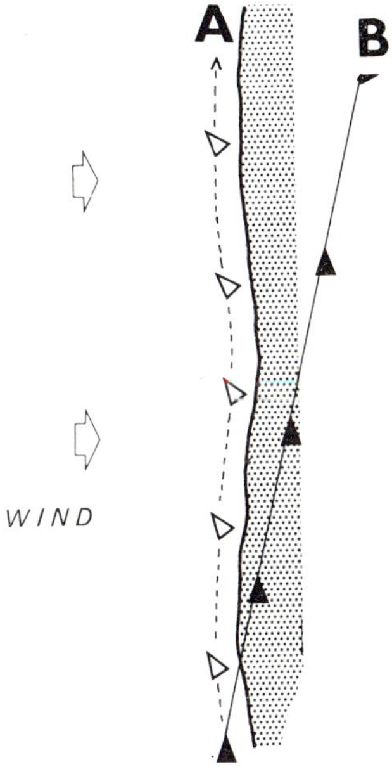

13.3. To track along a flight path parallel to the hill in a soaring wind the hang glider has to be headed partly into the wind. (A) If it is pointed along the hill the wind will cause it to drift over the ridge (B).

Continue flying along the ridge until you feel the lift weakening. If you are not sure where this ought to be, notice where other pilots are turning. Never go so far that the ridge changes direction or even shape as the lift may suddenly disappear or become wildly turbulent. (Fig. 13.5.) When you have decided on your turning-point allow the glider to drift back towards the slope slightly before actually making the turn. By doing this you ensure that when you have completed your turn you will be back, or very close to, your original track, although maybe higher. It is a rather tricky manoeuvre to get used to and many beginners either do not do it enough or at all, and fly out of the lift because they are too far out from the hill. If you do make this mistake you can still return to the correct track by allowing the turn to continue slightly until you have drifted back into the right position. (Fig. 13.6.)

13.4. After take-off turn to track along just upwind of the crest of the ridge.

But be careful if you are already sinking below the hilltop.

Once you have mastered 'beating the ridge' you will find that as long as you stay in the area of lift you will climb, until in due course you will have reached the ceiling for your particular bit of the ridge. Other pilots further along may be getting higher, and it will be tempting to go and join them. But think before you set off; there may be a gully between their bit of the hill and yours, or there may not be much in the way of landing places at the bottom.

As you gain height above the ridge you will find that the band of lift becomes wider, and that the top of the lift is further out from the hillface. As you climb you will be able to make each beat of the ridge slightly further out from the crest, giving you more freedom of manoeuvre.

13.5. A hill provides lift only when the wind is blowing more or less directly on to it. If a pilot flies along a ridge which changes direction he must expect the lift to disappear or the air to become turbulent.

If you are flying from a new site choose your take-off point carefully. Select a place as near to the edge that is smooth and will give you enough take-off run. If possible start near one end of the ridge so that when you take off and do your first turn you will have most of the ridge ahead of you. This will give you time to assess the lift, and still have time to think before having to turn again. If there is any cross-wind component, select the end that will make your first turn more into wind.

If you decide to take off below the crest of the ridge you may find that the wind sweeping up the hill, and trying to force itself between the hill and the rear of the rogallo, is causing the nose to pitch down. Do not attempt to deal with this situation yourself, as you will simply take off in a diving attitude. Ask another pilot to hold on to the forward wires and increase the angle of attack until you can

13.6. In light winds the band of lift may be very narrow and great care will be needed to stay within it.

feel the 'venturi' effect being cancelled. This may be much higher than the usual angle needed for take-off. When you no longer feel any nose-down pitching tendency give the command to release and take off in the usual manner. Be prepared to push yourself back quickly as the glider may still want to dive slightly. As soon as you are free of the effect of the slope check your speed again so that you do not fly too slowly.

These are the basic problems of soaring on a hill. It is a complex process so it is common sense not to rush matters. Once you have soared, and done so with only a normal amount of fear and excitement; not terrified because you cannot remember left from right and whether you were supposed to turn away from the ridge or what, you will really feel that you have accomplished something and flown like the birds. They, incidentally, are good indicators of smooth or gusty air, and show where the best lift is to be found.

Thermal soaring

On some warm summer days you may find yourself in unexpected surges of lift, or the steady slope lift will suddenly fluctuate with the wind altering its direction. The cause is probably thermal bubbles of warm air forming out in the valley and flowing up the face of the hill.

Thermals are the result of the sun warming the ground, which in turn warms the air in contact with it. This warming occurs only irregularly because some sorts of surface warm up more quickly than others. A dry ploughed field, for example, will warm up rapidly whereas a wood will need to sop up a lot of heat before it has become sufficiently warmed through to affect the temperature of the air above it. For this reason thermals may come off woods late in the day after upcurrents have ceased over open country. As the air over a thermal source warms it lessens in density compared to the surrounding air and starts to rise. As it rises it both expands and cools. When it has cooled to the same temperature as the surrounding air it ceases to rise further.

To begin with, a thermal will only go up very slowly and is, of course, also drifting along on the wind. If it forms well upwind of the soaring slope it may arrive at the ridge already higher than the top, and will be usable only by pilots already either near the top of the slope lift or who have used a previous thermal and still have some height left. If the source is closer to the hill it will arrive there below the top and flow up the face, probably accelerating as it does so. The effect of a thermal on the slope lift can be considerable because its passage causes air from all around to move in towards its invisible base. On both sides of the thermal the wind will temporarily swing inwards and blow along the slope. Downwind of the approaching thermal the slope wind may drop or even momentarily blow outwards from the hill. This can be very disconcerting if you do not appreciate what is happening. If you strike lucky and find yourself rising in what is obviously something more than slope lift, try to stay in it by S-turning outwards from the hill, or in a strong

13.7. If a thermal develops upwind of the hill it will drift along, rising up the face of the slope. Its passage will affect the local wind strength and direction.

wind just pointing into wind. If conditions are right and you are really high enough try to circle up in the lift. (Fig. 13.7.)

You will usually recognise the arrival of a thermal because your aircraft will surge up and accelerate temporarily as it gains energy from the lift. Do not be misled. If you fall out of a thermal, which is easy to do, you will lose energy and almost certainly lose some airspeed. Since the most likely way to fall out of a thermal is at the back—the downwind side—you could easily find yourself in rapidly sinking air behind the hill. Thermals are often marked by cumulus clouds at the top. These clouds occur when the rising, cooling thermal is no longer able to carry all the moisture contained in it. Condensation of some of this moisture takes place and a cumulus appears. If you get high in a thermal which seems to have no cloud-hat this may be because the air is very dry and the thermal is reaching its equilibrium temperature below the height at which condensation would take place; or it might be that you are going up in a young thermal the top of which has not yet reached cloudbase. In this case you may suddenly find the new cloud being born all around you.

The life of the small cumulus that grow at the top of thermals lasts only about 20 minutes and half of that time the cloud is actually dying away with no thermal underneath it, so only growing clouds are worth going for. Always try to work your way upwind of the hill with the height you gain from thermals, as this will give you the greatest freedom of manoeuvre to search for more lift. If you let yourself get drifted downwind all your spare height will have to be used to go back upwind to the hill again—unless you wish to fly cross-country.

Landing back on top

Landing on the hilltop saves a lot of walking and climbing, but just because you are higher than the crest does not automatically mean that a top landing is sensible. The landing area must be of sufficient size, of suitable contour—it can be very difficult on ridgeback hills—and clear of obstructions, because you are unlikely to be able to choose your landing place as precisely as you picked your take-off point. The other problem is that the place where you want to land may be in the slope lift zone, so that you remain airborne unable to get on to the ground.

As with the landing of all aircraft it is better to follow an approach pattern that will not only give you the best chance of success, but will enable you to 'go round again' if the landing spot is not so satisfactory after all. (Fig. 13.8.) The considerations are:

1 You are attempting to land in or through an area of lift.

2 As soon as your feet touch the ground the hang glider is relieved of your weight, and if the wind is strong it will immediately want to fly again.

3 To avoid landing with drift and possibly cartwheeling it is essential to land exactly into wind.

4 You need to avoid being blown or carried downwind of the hill crest into any lurking downdraught or curlover.

While you are soaring work out where you intend to land and how you will get there. Position yourself about 100 ft above the

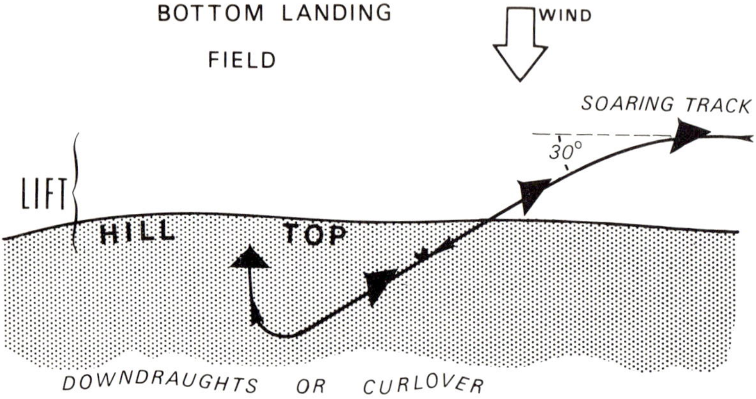

13.8. When landing on top of the hill start well to one side of your intended landing-point and allow yourself to track back over the hilltop, turning into wind at a height of about 25 ft.

hilltop and well to one side of the chosen landing place, so you are looking at it at an angle of about 30°. You will also need to be to windward of it—out from the hill—by about 30°. Up to this moment you have been pointing to some extent into wind in order to track along the hill. Now slightly alter your heading to track on a line to your landing place. This will bring you back gradually over the hill crest although you may still be flying within the lift band. You will now be moving faster over the ground, so check that you are maintaining your proper airspeed. As the lift decreases your sink rate will increase. When you are about 25 ft above the ground—a bit more than a rogallo standing on its wingtip—turn into wind. Your rate of descent may decrease again if, or as, you start to fly into increased lift. Keep absolutely into wind. At about 5 ft raise the nose slightly and as soon as your feet touch the ground, lower the nose firmly. If possible arrange with a friend to be around to grab the nose and help you get it down quickly.

If you make your final turn too high and find yourself going up, do not attempt to get on the ground anyhow. Soar until you can again position yourself correctly for a further complete approach.

Avoid allowing your approach path to drift you back over the hill at an angle greater than 30–35°, or you may find yourself either descending very fast, and, or, be unable to turn into wind in time before the ground arrives.

CHAPTER FOURTEEN

Gaining experience

The point to be made is that any flying is good for you. Just because you cannot soar don't think that there is nothing to be learnt. Even a straight flight to the bottom on a calm day can teach you something new. (Fig. 14.1.)

Conditions are never identical even from flight to flight, and it is the unpredictable vagaries of the elements that you will be challenging. The more you know of their behaviour the better pilot you will become. If you cannot fly on your home site try travelling to a new one, explore it and fly on it even if it is only a simple descent. Do not attempt too much too quickly. Become thoroughly proficient at every stage before going on to the next.

Prone harness

By now you will want to get the best performance out of your rogallo, and the simplest way is to reduce drag. This will improve both glide ratio and sinking speed. By flying with your body aligned with the airflow your drag is about one-fifth that of when it is vertical, because you are presenting only about 2 sq. ft to the airflow instead of 10 sq. ft. This equals a reduction of about 8 lb of drag, or an improvement in glide ratio from 1 : 4 to 1 : 4.5 and sink speed from 2 m/sec to perhaps 1.75 m/sec. This is not much but may be just enough to make the difference between staying up in marginal lift, or getting across a gully to a better ridge beyond.

A prone harness can allow you to get into trouble more easily because of the greater amount that you can shift your weight, but in capable hands it permits better and more accurate control; further, you have more control over the amount of drag that you present to the airflow. By moving between the vertical and prone positions the steepness of the descent path can be modified. The harness must be such that it will freely allow a stand-up take-off

14.1. Something can be learnt from every flight. Even a simple descent into a strange field adds to the pilot's experience.

14.2. A prone harness must be well designed and made, have support for the legs, and allow the pilot to swing quickly to and from the vertical position.

and a rapid return to the vertical for landing. It must also have proper support for the legs as well as the body so that you can remain fully prone without becoming tired quickly. If you find yourself slowly slipping back to the vertical the harness is not doing its job. With a prone harness you may find it tiring to hold your head up for long periods and need to return to the vertical from time to time to give your neck a rest. Try to do this where the lift is good. (Fig. 14.2.) The length of a prone, or supine, harness has to be such that it will give the equivalent lateral stability and control to a vertical one, so do not experiment without advice from the manufacturer. The control frame will need to be lengthened and moved forward, and your harness be of a length that will keep your body just clear of the bar.

Emergency landings: trees and water

Sometimes the situation is misjudged and there is no alternative to landing in trees or on water.

Trees. Choose the softest looking densest mass of trees, such as firs, in preference to large isolated trees like oaks. Land into wind and as slowly as possible, dropping gently and near vertically on to the top of them. Keep your legs together, draw your knees and body into a ball and protect your face by tucking in your chin and hunching your shoulders. Shut your mouth.

Water. Lakes are often smooth, but the sea may have steep waves. In neither case is it advisable to release yourself from your harness before touching the water. Over glassy water it may not be possible to judge your height to nearer than 100 ft, which is an undesirable altitude to fall out of your harness. Relieved of your weight, even at 5–10 ft, the wing is likely to drop more heavily upon you than when it is attached.

On a lake land into wind near the downwind shore so that you will be drifted there. On the sea, also land into wind or nearly so, but if there is a big or heavy swell land on the back of the rising swell, near but behind the crest. If you land in the trough or on the face of the swell, waves may break on top of you. As soon as you are in the water detach yourself from the rogallo. Unclipping your harness from the control frame may be the quickest way. The wing will probably blow over backwards, leaving you clear, but if it does not and you find you are under the wing, don't panic. Take your time. There will be several pockets of air trapped under the sail. Pushing it up will probably move one towards you. Breath well a few times while looking at the sail to see how it lies above you, and where the bracing wires are, and then decide the best way to get out from underneath. Take a deep breath and dive or pull yourself along one of the tubes, whichever seems best. When clear of the wing stay near it, unless land is *very* close and you are certain that you can swim the distance. It will be easier for people looking for you to see a wing rather than a very small head.

Unless the tubes are blocked at the ends the wing will probably soon sink, unless a great deal of air got trapped underneath. Try to keep yourself afloat by trapping air in your helmet or clothes.

Cold and fatigue

When you are making flights of an hour or more, it is as well to know and recognise the symptoms of cold and fatigue. Because you are enjoying the flying your senses become dulled to the gradual cold and exhaustion your body and mind will be suffering;

it is quite an energetic sport apart from the climbs to the top of the hill!

You usually become aware of cold before anything else, apart from numbness perhaps in your legs and associated regions. But even on a summer day you can become quite chilly. In winter it is a constant and severe problem, and coupled with fatigue it is your worst enemy.

Although hang gliding is not dangerous if you are sensible you have to devote your entire attention to it, because any lack of concentration in the air is potentially lethal. If you are soaring with little effort the flight, after a while, becomes boring as well as enjoyable—even to the keenest pilot. Often, however, the prospect of being able to boast about a long flight keeps you going. This is when the problem of cold becomes real. If you are aware that your hands and feet are cold and your eyes are watering, they are obviously distracting your attention. Without realising it you have become physically and mentally fatigued. You may be wishing that some feeling would return to your fingers and that you had brought a cushion, and you suddenly find yourself in a turn with too little airspeed because your concentration has gone.

A sudden gust swings you towards the slope and you have an emergency on your hands and so ends that flight, because your reactions were too slow to effect a recovery. When the conditions look good for a long flight always wear more clothing than seems necessary. Although you may be hot when you take off, this will not last long. Gloves are essential in all weathers because you are holding a metal control frame that is always cold.

If you find yourself becoming bored but still want to go on flying set yourself some simple tasks to keep your mind alert: find out exactly how high you can get, decide that you are going to turn precisely over that clump of grass, etc.

Always land at the first signs of cold, fatigue or loss of concentration. You can be on the ground for a warm-up within minutes. If you wait and prolong the flight until you are extremely cold, it always seems to take longer to get down than you expect, and invariably you will end with a poor, untidy landing.

CHAPTER FIFTEEN

360° turns

The manoeuvre most abused by insufficiently skilled pilots—and some skilled ones—is the 360° turn, which in a rogallo demands not only a proper understanding of what is involved but skill of a high order. Go on learning more about your aircraft and how it flies, about the more complex aspects of control and the forces involved. Without this knowledge you do not know what you are really trying to do; with it, the reasons for control movements are clear and you have an intelligent understanding of the whole problem.

When you have done a few hours' soaring, are capable of staying up in light winds and weak lift, and can turn accurately and economically at each end of your beat along the ridge, you may become increasingly tempted to do a 360. Before you do, remember that it is not an essential manoeuvre for any sort of rogallo slope soaring, that you should have at least 500 ft of height above a big hill that is providing plentiful smooth lift, and that before you start you should be really well out ahead of the hill. You should also be honest with yourself and decide whether your rogallo really does have the same controllability as the others that you have seen do 360s.

When you do your first 360 you will be faced with no less than three new aspects of flying, so you will have to learn, and get right, three new things at once:

1. That for half of the 360 you will be flying more or less downwind fast over the ground, which you have probably never done before.
2. That in a turn the stalling speed increases, so does the sinking speed. So you come down faster.
3. Finally, you will have to learn how to control a continuous turn without either going into a spiral dive or stalling.

Flying downwind

If you could do a 360 in completely calm conditions you would fly a circle both in the air and over the ground. The diameter of this circle would be a little over 30 metres flying at an airspeed of 20 mph. This situation is unlikely to occur, except from a balloon drop or in the Alps, as without slope soaring you are unlikely to have sufficient height, and when soaring there will be a wind of some 15–20 mph. Figure 15.1 shows the same *air* circle that would have been flown in the calm conditions, showing the path of the aircraft *over the ground* in a fresh wind. It is obvious that without enough height you will hit the hill. Even with just enough height you could be in the turbulent air behind the crest, and easily lose control of the situation.

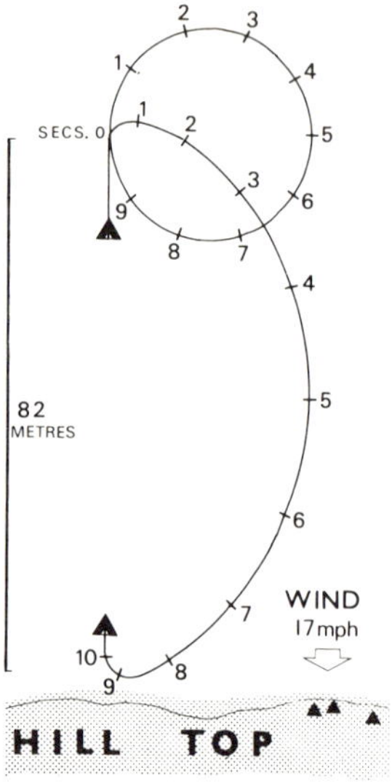

15.1. A well-flown 360° turn in no wind is a circle in the air *and* over the ground. In a fresh wind the same *air* circle describes a different track over the ground. Appreciable height may be lost in the turn.

Controlling the turn

Although you can turn accurately while slope soaring along the ridge, these turns, which do not usually require even a 180° change of direction, give insufficient time for any real faults to develop—and show their teeth.

To understand exactly what happens when the rogallo turns, it will probably be useful to first of all go through a simple 90° turn step by step:

1 You are flying straight at the proper airspeed and angle of attack.

2 You shift your weight to one side, the wing banks and starts to slip towards the direction of the inner (lower) wing. This causes an asymmetric flow across the sail.

3 This asymmetric flow causes the nose of the aircraft to turn or yaw in the direction of the inner wing. This is because the deeper billow at the rear end of the sail produces a weather-cock effect.

4 The rogallo is now turning but in an increasingly nose-down attitude. In a 90° turn this effect will have become barely noticeable before you shift your weight once more to level the wings. If the nose is slightly down you will correct this automatically, without perhaps realising how it got there, particularly if the air is at all turbulent.

When you do a 360 you will have this nose-down effect all the way around the circle, unless you correct it by pushing out on the control frame to move your weight back. If you do a really steep 360 you may even run out of 'nose-up' control.

When you are banked steeply for more than a few seconds you may get the idea that the rogallo is no longer controllable in a normal sense. It is, of course, but you have got used to thinking of controlling the aircraft in relation to the horizon; when you move your body weight back you expect the nose to go higher in relation to the horizon. When the aircraft is steeply banked pushing out still makes the nose go up, but 'up' is now somewhere between the vertical and the horizontal. Pushing the body back will now, therefore, help increase the *rate* of turn, as well as help raise the nose. For the same reason keeping your weight towards the inside of the turn will

15.2. A competition slalom gives excellent practice in learning how to control the turn, but do not become ambitious too quickly.

not make you turn faster, but merely slip downwards. (Fig. 15.2.) It will be necessary to adjust your position in order to keep the bank constant.

Increase in stalling speed

The stall speed increases in a turn because the wing has to carry not only the normal weight of the aircraft, but the extra weight or loading caused by centrifugal force. The increase is negligible in a gentle change of direction but goes up rapidly as the rate and steepness of the turn increases, so that by the time you are doing a 360 at about 60° of bank, your stall speed will be nearly one and a half times greater than in straight flight, so you will have to increase speed for the turn, and as you fly faster the drag will increase.

This it will do increasingly rapidly—it goes up as the square of the speed. This extra drag will, of course, lower the lift/drag ratio, reducing the performance of the rogallo, and causing you to descend more rapidly. This is why you need all that spare height. You are learning to control your rogallo in a new and difficult manoeuvre, while it is descending faster than usual, and at the same time being perhaps swept rapidly towards the hill.

Flying the 360

If you must do a 360 follow this checklist carefully:

1 Make sure the hill and the weather are suitable. The lift should be strong, smooth, and extend 100 metres or more out ahead of the hill and support you at least 500 ft above the top. Or the hill should be big enough to allow you to get at least 250 metres from the nearest ground in any direction without the aid of slope lift.

2 Get yourself as high as possible and as far out ahead of the ridge as you can, and have a good look-out for other pilots. If possible you should have warned them in advance that you might be flying a 360.

3 Increase speed slightly to help look after the higher stall speed and to improve controllability.

4 Bank the wing firmly and fairly steeply with the normal lateral weight shift.

5 Keep the nose from going down and the aircraft from descending in a spiral by pushing the body weight back as much as seems necessary. If you are prone be sure to push out and not press down!

6 When you are flying downwind expect to be moving very fast over the ground. Do not interpret this as necessarily having too high an airspeed. Resist the natural tendency to slow the aircraft. Check your airspeed by the noise the wing is making and by the position of the nose in relation to the horizon; it should at least be travelling steadily around it.

7 When you are coming round into wind once more level the wings, and pull yourself forward on the control frame to prevent the nose going up and the aircraft stalling.

8 If the turn gets out of control and speed is rising as you spiral earthwards, immediately reduce the amount of bank. If you still feel out of control come out of the turn completely and sort yourself out. Do not try experimenting with some bright idea at a groundspeed of 60 mph. This is why you must have a lot of spare height. A rogallo in a good 360 may lose about 75–100 ft, and when not very well flown the height loss may be 150 ft or more. Remember that during the turn the sail will be clean and quiet because of the higher loading due to centrifugal force, and because your weight being back will have also moved the centre of pressure back. If, however, you run out of nose-up control the sail will become noisy. If, through some disastrous error, and it will be disastrous if you find yourself heading downwind towards the hillface, flare for a landing as hard and as fully as you can in plenty of time before you hit. It is not much of a chance but about the only one you have got.

CHAPTER SIXTEEN

Instruments

As the performance of hang gliders, and your skill, improves you will want to fly with greater accuracy and suitable instruments will help you to do this; but do not expect any instruments to provide a short cut to expertise. When you are flying close to the ground changes in height are readily noticeable, and instruments are likely to do little except distract your attention from the actual flying. When soaring at greater heights it is not so easy to judge either how high above the ground you are or whether you are climbing or descending. Speed on a hang glider can be more readily assessed by the sound and feel of the wing regardless of height, so an airspeed indicator is unneccessary until or unless you are flying a hang glider with a wide speed range and want to fly it within 1–2 mph of a given speed.

Variometer

This is the most useful instrument as it tells you if you are going up or down. The instrument (Fig. 16.1) works by registering the rate of change of the barometric pressure either visually in terms of indications against a scale, such as metres/second up or down, or as sound. For hang gliders the audio variometer is more useful; it does not require watching and therefore does not have to be fitted in front of the pilot—it can go in a pocket as long as you can hear the undulating note. This rises in pitch when the glider is rising and descends when it is sinking. The variometer will only give an accurate reading of rise and sink when the aircraft is flown at a steady speed. Dives, climbs and gusts will result temporarily in false readings. The variometer can be connected to a total-energy device on the aircraft which will virtually eliminate the effect of speed changes and gusts. Most conventional gliders are so fitted because they operate over a very wide speed range.

16.1. Variometer fitted to hang glider control frame. On left is a stopwatch and on right an altimeter.

Altimeter

The altimeter, which is not at present frequently used, is simply a barometer with the pressure indicated in feet of altitude instead of millibars or inches of mercury. Being a barometer the reading will change as the pressure of the air changes so that if, for example, the pressure is lowering with the approach of a depression, the altimeter will increasingly over-read and show you height that you have not got. For hang gliding these errors are unimportant when slope soaring in clear air. Before take-off the altimeter should be set either at zero on the hilltop when it will indicate height reached above the hill, or it can be set at the actual height of the hilltop, say 500 ft, in which case it will indicate heights reached above sea-level.

Airspeed indicator

This instrument, also not yet in common use, indicates the speed of the aircraft through the air. It does not tell you your speed over the ground except in a flat calm. Airspeed indicators are subject to position, or pressure, errors which may be large if the pitot head is close under the sail or is disturbed by the flow around the pilot's body.

Ground instruments

Before flying, particularly on a strange site it is useful to know the strength and direction of the wind and the degree of steepness of the slope. A hand-held wind-strength meter, such as the ventimeter, is always useful, because it is possible to get an idea of the gustiness of the air as well. (Figs. 16.2 a and b.) However, this is a much-abused instrument, being relied upon too often. It should be used as a check on your own assessment of the wind. Such instruments may give their indication as a force on the Beaufort scale or in miles per hour.

Since an instrument is not infallible, or may have been left behind, it is sensible to always try to assess the windspeed by its feel, its noise and by the movement of grass or trees yourself, then use the instrument to check your guess. A compass helps to determine the extent to which a slope curves or bends as well as giving the direction it faces. It will also help you decide which hill to go to by giving an accurate check on the surface wind. A glide-slope indicator can be helpful in determining whether a new slope is or is not steep enough. It is not an essential instrument because even if your eye is not a good enough guide you can supply yourself with the angle of slope by using a school protractor upside down against the horizon, or even folding a square piece of paper to give you angles of, say, 45° or 22½°.

Instruments can be useful, but never think a rogallo hung about with instruments like a Christmas tree will be more efficient. Because you are having to divide your attention you will probably fly less well, and instruments can, and do, go wrong.

16.2. a & b. Ventimeter. A simple and reliable instrument to indicate the direction of the wind and its strength. The position of the vane rising up the tube indicates windspeed.

CHAPTER SEVENTEEN

What next?

Most pilots learn to fly on a rogallo because it is simple, inexpensive, and robust. One of its merits for this purpose is that it has a steep glide path so that while you are learning to control the hang glider in the air you are not also floating across the countryside; the field directly ahead of you is where you are going.

Positioning yourself in the air becomes important, of course, as soon as you start to soar, but by then you will, or should, be well on the way to mastering the art of making your aircraft do what you want it to. Soaring a hang glider, whether in slope lift or thermal, is very satisfying because each flight is somehow different from the last even on the same hill. The wind, visibility, temperature and the hang gliders you are flying with all combine to make each flight a new and exhilarating experience. However, in due course, the desire for a better-performance hang glider either becomes very important to you, or ideas for new designs start to keep you awake at night. You realise that the home slope is becoming too crowded, but you do not have quite a good enough glide ratio to reach the next stretch of hill, or you go up in a thermal but cannot reach those other gliders obviously flying in better lift. So you look around for something better—and find a bewildering array of new hang gliders ranging from flexible sailwings of 'aeroplane' planform to rigidly constructed flying wings with no tail at all. Almost all of these aircraft have one thing in common; an immediate jump in glide ratio from the 1:4 of an ordinary rogallo to 1:8 or better. Not only can more slopes or better thermals be reached but the hills themselves do not need to be quite so steep. But you never get something for nothing. Not only will you have to make more decisions and develop better judgement about choosing landing areas and getting down safely in them, but you will need to obtain a proper understanding of the flying and control differences between these more advanced hang gliders and the basic rogallo.

17.1. The Swallowtail. Some rogallos have a cutaway trailing edge to increase the aspect ratio. The tail 'sting' helps directional stability and the tip battens control washout.

17.2. Tweetie. An Australian semi-rigid aerofoil hang glider with a glide ratio of about 8 : 1. The construction uses marine parts and fittings and the sail is fully battened to retain the aerofoil shape.

You know that a rogallo sail takes up its aerofoil shape and provides lift only when the airflow is moving past it with the wing at a positive angle of attack. If the angle of attack is reduced too much the sail will luff, undulate, and provide insufficient lift together with loss of control. This cannot happen if the wing is rigidly constructed (like the wing of a conventional glider or aeroplane) and it is almost impossible in an otherwise flexible single-surface wing with fixed preformed battens. It does not mean that there are no dive problems; they are just different ones. They come under the heading of high-speed flight—which from time to time you may feel tempted to indulge in once you get a super ship.

Flying fast or too fast

All conventional aircraft have a speed above which they may not be flown because the structure could no longer cope with the loads imposed upon it. The maximum permitted speed, sometimes called redline, or *Vne*, is the maximum speed that the designer has allowed for in his calculations. Certainly you can have an aircraft with a higher redline speed if you want one, but it will be heavier or more expensive, or both. On a hang glider, which is very light, and as

17.3. Quicksilver (*l.*) of rigid construction with a single-surface aerofoil and (*r.*) an experimental Seagull V fitted with a fin.

17.4. An experimental modification of Tweetie. The tailed hang glider usually needs a helper to hold up the tail for take-off.

cheap as possible, the maximum permitted speed is low. The hang glider is, after all, intended for flying around slowly over hills.

The real risk in mistakenly overspeeding a rigid or semi-rigid wing hang glider is that you probably do not know what is the redline speed, and even if you did, you do not have an accurate airspeed indicator. In practice, the risk of exceeding the maximum permitted speed is probably small because as you increase speed the drag goes up rapidly—double the speed and you have four times the drag; and as the drag goes up the performance of the aircraft goes down, and so do you. The most likely chance of getting

17.5. Easy Riser. A swept tailless biplane which breaks down into a small enough package to be carried on a car roof-rack.

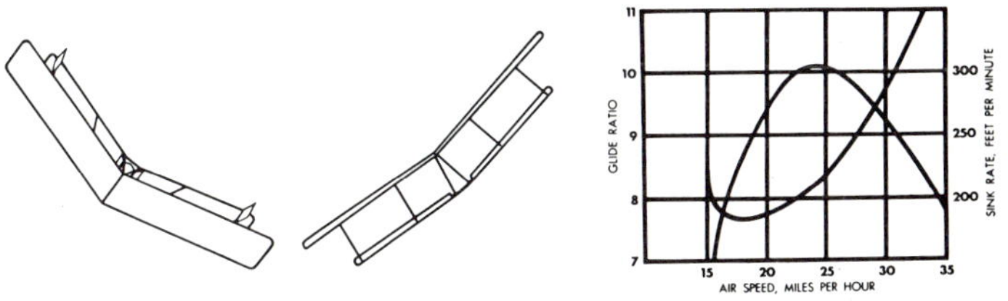

Performance

Speed range	16-45
Take-off air speed	17
Landing air speed approach	20-25
Landing air speed, flare out	4-6
Stall speed	16
Best glide speed	23-24
Minimum sink speed	18-20
Sink rate minimum	180
Glide ratio maximum	10+
Glide ratio minimum	1.0
Bank angle	60°+
Control response	FAST

Dimensions

Wing span (trailing edge)	30
Wing area sq. ft.	170
Aspect ratio main wing	8.8
Wing loading lb/ft²	1.0-1.47
Chord	41"
Airfoil	LM 7610
Sweep	15°
Weight lb.	50
Pilot wt. max. lb.	200
Design 'g' load	5.0
Ultimate 'g' load	7.5
Folded size	18" x 45" x 16 ft.
Pilot cockpit	tube support with optional swing seat
Pitch/speed control	weight shift
Roll/yaw control	drag rudders
Speed limiting	cables, struts, & drag brakes

into structural failure trouble is when trying to penetrate against a very strong wind in wildly turbulent air, because you got caught out by the weather.

The stall

At the slow-speed end of the scale, at the stall, the behaviour of the ordinary delta rogallo and hang gliders with longer, higher aspect-ratio wings is also different. The rogallo generally has an indeterminate mushy type of stall with the wing behaving more like a parachute. On a long rigid wing with a substantially straight leading edge the stall will be more definite. This is because it occurs more uniformly along the wing leading edge and this causes the nose to drop in a more positive manner. The stalled aircraft will fall in a diving attitude until enough speed for the wing to fly again has been gained. Height, of course, will be lost, and although on a light

17.6. Fulmar, a semi-rigid hang glider with aileron controls to assist in turning.

hang glider this may be as little as 20 ft or so you may, at this moment, have less than this height above the ground.

A long-winged hang glider is also more likely to drop a wing at the stall than is a rogallo, especially if the aircraft is turning or yawing, since one wing will be flying more slowly than the other and will stall first. This is the classic situation that has resulted in many conventional aircraft spinning in on the approach to land. However, very slow-speed aircraft need only very little additional speed to unstall the wings, so any wing drop can usually be caught in time by an aware pilot, even with body shift control, unless the aircraft is stalled while turning in a wind gradient. Then it may not be possible to regain enough speed while falling through the decelerating airflow close to the ground.

Most 'acroplane' plan-form and rigid tailless hang gliders will have a certain amount of washout, or twist, designed into the wings, so that any stall in straight flight will start at the centre and not at the tips. This will reduce any wing-drop tendencies. Most slow-speed aircraft have gentle stall characteristics and may be difficult to persuade to drop their nose at all. But do not be misled. All fixed-wing aircraft *will* stall, and will also do so more readily if the weight of the pilot is too far aft, so that the centre of gravity is aft of that intended by the designer.

Controls

Control of a hang glider can be achieved in a number of different ways, in addition to pilot weight shift, as on the ordinary rogallo. On hang gliders of other shape and construction pitch control—for climbing and diving—may be by weight shift with a rudder, or tip draggers, to induce the yaw needed for turning; or there may be control surfaces in all the three planes of pitch, roll, and yaw. The roll control may be in the form of ordinary ailerons, wingtip spoilers or rudders, or even with wing warping.

The advantage of control by weight shift only is that the hang glider can be made simpler, cheaper, and easier to maintain because there are fewer moving parts. The disadvantage is that control may be less positive, more tiring, and with a longer wing less effective in roll, so that it is more difficult to turn. Although it is possible to induce a turn only with yaw considerable drag will be produced so that the aircraft will lose some height. If the pilot is not able to sufficiently roll the hang glider into the turn he will not be able to take full advantage of its performance.

Whatever system of control is built in to the better-performance hang glider, it is important that the pilot understands exactly how the turn is being achieved. On an ordinary rogallo the pilot moves his weight to the side he wants to turn—say, to the left. This causes an asymmetric flow across the wing with the deep billow towards the rear acting as the weathercock. This swings the nose into the direction that the aircraft is slipping—to the left. On a tailed hang glider, such as Tweetie, or Gulp, the asymmetric flow caused by the slip to the left acts on the vertical fin to weathercock the aircraft into the turn. What is being achieved is a turn produced by a roll and slip-induced yaw. With a hang glider, such as Quicksilver, the vertical tail surface is a movable rudder. When the pilot wants to turn he puts on rudder to produce yaw and shifts his body weight in the same direction to produce roll and slip. The effect of the rudder is to yaw the aircraft so that the nose swings round. This causes the outer wing to move faster through the air giving it more lift and helping the hang glider to roll into a properly banked turn. This is a turn initially produced by yaw-induced roll. On a swept tailless aircraft, such as the Fledgling or Icarus V, which has vertical tip draggers at each wingtip, the turn is initiated by deflecting the dragger surface to slow down the inner wing. This causes differential lift on the two wings, inducing roll and slip. Pilot weight shift speeds the effect.

The third method of control, easiest on rigid-wing hang gliders, is by normal 'aeroplane' control surfaces, examples being the VJ-23 and VJ-24. Such an arrangement of controls naturally makes conversion to hang gliding easier for the conventional aeroplane or glider pilot, since the controls are working in the sense that he is used to—moving the stick forward for nose-down, etc. Such pilots

17.7. Breenwave. An experimental flexible wing tailless with tip draggers being flown supine. Note variometer on the control frame.

often have difficulty initially with control by weight shift since movements seem to them to be in the wrong sense—moving the arms forward does not make the nose go down, but up. It would be better if the conventional pilot could instead think in terms of weight forward for nose-down, but it is not always easy to change ingrained habits quickly.

Although control of a hang glider with normal control surfaces is easier for the conventional pilot, he may find that control in roll is poorer than he expected, or indeed as might be found by a rogallo pilot. This is because the vertical hang position of the pilot puts his weight well below the wings creating a pendulum stability effect. If he is not used to weight shift control he may do little or nothing to help his aircraft develop roll.

Although on longer-winged hang gliders roll control has to be helped by some yaw-inducing surface such as a rudder, control in pitch is not a problem. On all known types of hang glider control in the fore and aft sense by body shift is not only adequate but easy to achieve. Human arms push and pull well and the hands are good in grip and sensitivity.

The thought of better performance—the ability to glide further and soar in less strong conditions—is attractive, but it demands greater critical judgement from the pilot. There is now a choice, or several choices, of where the hang glider can go and where it will be landed. More decisions have to be made, and all of them in time. The flatter glide means that either a larger place is needed for landing, or the landing has to be made with greater accuracy. Spoilers can be used as an approach control, as on the Icarus V, by deflecting both tip draggers at the same time but in opposed directions.

With the somewhat improved speed range of the higher-performance hang glider, the commodity of speed can be traded to a limited extent for distance not only when soaring but to improve control over the approach path. This is particularly the case when there is a wind. If, when headed into the wind, the hang glider is flown a little more slowly it will be descending while not making much progress over the ground, but having a steeper effective approach path. If it is flown faster it will make better headway against the wind.

The technique of landing up a slope is also somewhat different to doing so in an ordinary rogallo. The need with a more conventional type of wing is to have enough reserve of speed to be able to flare through the additional angle caused by the slope. In a rogallo, if this extra speed is not available the aircraft may just sink rather heavily on to the ground. (Fig. 17.7.) A rigid wing without enough speed will be more likely to thump into the ground if it is very low, or stall nose-down. This is likely to result in damage which will take time to repair.

Towing

As newer and better hang gliders are built, it is probable that there will be an increasing interest in towed launches, if only to get airborne where there are no hills. There are many reasons why the standard rogallo should not be towed. If the rope breaks, the wing is likely to flip over on its back; even if the tow is merely too fast the pilot may not be able to prevent the nose going right up so that when he comes off the top of the launch he may either go over on his back or whip stall. Even if the location of the vertical bridle towing-points are carefully worked out, the towing of ordinary rogallos can be

17.8. Some new hang gliders start life as radio-controlled models to see if the idea works.

a high-risk activity. It is not yet suitable for training, which is what towing will be mainly needed for. Also, the flight may be uneconomically short. Slope-soaring hills are the place for rogallos, where they provide really good flying.

With some of the newer, better-performance hang gliders, particularly those with rigid wings the situation is somewhat different. If designed for the job and towed at a suitably slow speed the improved glide ratio will give enough flight time for a simple circuit, and flat site training could become practicable. Weight shift control is not really adequate to deal with towed launches by inexperienced pilots if the intention is to obtain height, although dual flying could be the answer. Some wind would, of course, be necessary if the pilot were not to have to run so fast that he would fall flat on his face before getting airborne. In Sweden towing is carried out from frozen lakes with the pilot on skis.

The future

The future holds great promise for hang gliding. It is one of the few areas of aviation where it is still possible for an individual to design, build and fly his own aircraft. But unlike conventional aircraft the hang glider designer is working far nearer the frontiers of knowledge, because he is combining the extremes in light construction, slow speed, different methods of control, and the use of new-found materials often all at the same time. His problem is further complicated by the almost complete lack of instrumentation for test-flying evaluation. The pitch stability of flying 'plank' wings, for example, is complex, and several hours of test flying with nothing going wrong does not mean that a different combination of pilot weight and turbulence will also be free of trouble. A great deal is now known about how to make a good rogallo, but the search for better-performance hang gliders requires greater technical knowledge and more research time. It should not be expected to happen overnight.

Perhaps the first need of the new designer is to carefully consider priorities in the specification of his dream-ship. The most important early decision that he has to take is whether he wants one man handling and cartop portability, or whether in the interests of performance he is prepared to accept the need for a crew and even a trailer in order to fly. This will determine the method of construction, and almost certainly the method of control. Since one-man portability has much to recommend it to the pilot brought up on a rogallo, the designer will need to study the best ways of obtaining a high aspect-ratio wing of good aerofoil shape that can also be rolled up, and is structurally stiff enough.

This is an intriguing problem which no one yet has fully solved. Given the right brains and energy, it would be possible in a very few years to produce a hang glider with a glide ratio of 1 : 15 and one-man portability. This is the next goal.

17.9. Gulp, a roll-up semi-rigid of British design. It can be rigged in 2 minutes.

APPENDIX ONE

The hang glider pilot's Code of Practice

The intention of the Code is to set a standard of behaviour that should be followed by all pilots. We cannot expect the goodwill, help and encouragement of the authorities and the public unless we clearly demonstrate that we are responsible and able to maintain a high standard of safety and control.

The site

1 Ensure that the permission of the landowner, occupier or authority has been obtained before using a site.

When seeking permission to fly always present your Association membership card and pilot certificate. Ensure your third-party insurance is valid.

State exactly where you wish to fly and where you intend to land.

When visiting sites administered by other operators contact them in advance, and observe their local rules.

Do not fly from a site where livestock are having their young—usually in the spring. Check with the farmer.

2 Inform the local police if your flying activities are likely to cause traffic congestion.

Drive considerately—you are easily identified with your wing on the roof.

Park your car with consideration for others. Find a proper parking place, not the grass road verge or the site itself.

Use only recognised gates and paths. Do not climb over walls, fences, or go through hedges.

Always close gates and do not let animals escape while you are using a gate.

Designate take-off and landing areas and keep these free of spectators and parked hang gliders.

Always park into wind and do not leave a rigged hang glider unattended.

If model fliers are using the site come to an amicable arrangement for sharing the air, they are just as interested in flying as you are.

3 Dogs should not be taken on to the site without the landowner's permission, and then must be kept under control.

Avoid landing in standing crops. If you do, keep other people out and carry your wing out along the rows to do minimum damage.

Report *any* damage to the landowner.

Do not leave litter.

Remember, a single inconsiderate act can lose a complete site for everyone.

Flying

Any fool can fly a hang glider—but not for long. Learn the right mental attitude. For most of our lives a lot of people are looking after us so we can make a lot of mistakes and it does not matter too much. Take off in a hang glider and you are on your own; make a mistake and you will pay for it. It may only mean a bruise or loss of pride, but you *never* get away with it entirely.

It takes a number of poor flights or a crash, or both, before this sinks in but until it does you are a fool in a hang glider and you will not be flying it much longer.

You should always know what could happen next. If you do not you are taking chances. Don't take chances.

4 *Your glider.* It should be of approved design and manufacture. If secondhand get it checked by the manufacturer or a safety officer.

Carry out periodic checks and replace doubtful or damaged components.

Always check thoroughly after a heavy landing.

If building to plans get the finished aircraft checked by the designer or a safety officer. Always refer to the designer or manufacturer before making modifications.

Ensure that your hang glider is the correct size for your height and weight.

5 *Equipment.* Never fly without a crash helmet. It should fit properly and not impair your hearing. Remove visors and peaks.

Boots should give support and sure footing when landing or climbing uphill. Avoid boots with lacing hooks, they can snag and kill.

Gloves should keep your hands warm, give protection on landing and not slip on the control frame.

6 *Before flying.* Join your local association, school or club, and get proper training. You will learn more quickly with a good instructor.

Never accept advice from anyone unless you have seen him fly or can ascertain his qualifications. Never go flying on your own.

Get a weather forecast and learn the site wind characteristics.

Carry out a pre-flight check of your aircraft and equipment before every flight.

7 *Your general flying.* Beware of how easy others make it look. It isn't. If there are other aircraft on the ridge or spectators on the ground:

Don't fly unnecessarily over the take-off and landing areas.

Don't fly low over spectators or show off.

Don't fly erratically about. Try to adopt a pattern that will be predictable to other pilots. Keep a good look-out at all times.

Don't be a lift hog, sitting in it and keeping others out.

If the number of hang gliders flying has to be limited to avoid overcrowding, don't take more than your fair share of time.

After landing remove your aircraft as quickly as possible from the landing area.

8 *Accidents.* If there is serious personal injury to a pilot the accident must be reported to the police without delay. You must also inform your association so that future similar accidents may be avoided.

Aviation in itself is not inherently dangerous, but it is terribly unforgiving of any carelessness, incapacity or neglect.

—Said in 1920 and still true today.

APPENDIX TWO

Fédération Aeronautique Internationale

FAI Delta Bronze hang glider pilot badge

The pilot must make a flight, officially observed, as follows: A distance of not less than 2 km must be flown over a course of not less than 0.5 km between turning points. A controlled landing must be made within 25 metres of a designated spot.

Delta Silver badge

Distance: a straight flight of at least 50 km.

Height: a gain of height of at least 1,000 metres.

Duration: a flight of 5 hrs.

Tests may be carried out separately or in the same flight and in any country. Applications for FAI badges are made through BHGA.

Addresses

British Hang Gliding Association,
Monksilver, Taunton, Somerset, England.

Publishes *Wings!* Supplies information on Pilot grading, lists of clubs and membership of the BHGA.

United States Hang Gliding Association Inc.,
Box 66306, Los Angeles, CA 90066, USA.

Publishes *Hang Gliding*.

APPENDIX THREE

First Aid

1 When flying off big hills or cliffs you may have to cope with an accident without much help. It does not actually need a hang glider; people fall off high places with monotonous regularity using only smooth-soled shoes as a means of propulsion. So what do you do?

If the casualty is attached to a hang glider, detach him before he blows away, but without moving his head, back, or limbs, if there is any chance of bone damage. Avoid rotating or bending forward neck or back.

2 People must breathe, so loosen clothes around neck, and if unconscious see nothing obstructs nose and throat—including tongue.

3 Send for medical help if even partly unconscious, if there is bad bleeding, any bones broken, internal pain, difficulty in breathing, or if for *any other reason* you feel all is not well. Give your message clearly saying what is needed and *where you are.* The local police or coastguard can quickly locate '¼ mile S of the Beacon' but may waste valuable time searching 'up on the hill over there'. If you give a grid reference, write it down.

4 Protect casualty from wind and keep him from getting cold. Do not make him too hot and keep sun off his face and head. Loosen waistbelt and other tight clothing. If ankles damaged loosen boots but do not remove them.

5 Reassure casualty and be relaxed yourself. Observe carefully for signs of back injury and limb movement. Do not ask him to wiggle his toes—you will scare him if he cannot. Drive away spectators and agitated friends.

6 If bleeding badly raise limb if it is not broken and apply pressure with fingers on the heart side of injury. You have two hands, use both to try to find the right place. If first aid kit available put sterile pad on or around the wound and press that. Do not use a tourniquet except as a last resort and then slacken it briefly every few minutes. Heads bleed readily, try to slow bleeding with casualty horizontal.

7 Do not give the casualty anything at all to drink or eat if there is any possibility of head or internal injuries, otherwise he can be given a little water if he is thirsty.

8 If the injuries are severe or there is much blood loss, shock or delayed shock will occur, with pallor, cold clammy skin and increased heart rate. If injuries are slight the casualty may insist he is all right and want to fly again. Discourage this; although some active people know well what bumps and bruises they can cope with, newcomers to the sport may not.

9 If the casualty has been in water and appears drowned carry clear of tide and empty mouth of water, seaweed, etc. Lay on ground holding head back to clear airway and give mouth-to-mouth resuscitation. You may have to go on doing this for a long time so breathe in a way that is natural to yourself. If you severely modify your own breathing rate you may become breathless yourself. Develop a smooth rhythm. If no pulse and you are alone give external cardiac massage. You cannot do both at once so give about ten breaths (about $\frac{1}{2}$ minute) then fifteen deep springy presses at heart-beat rhythm (about 15 seconds), and continue in this way. If a helper turns up get him to do one continuously while you do the other. Do not stop. When casualty starts to breathe himself turn on his side and watch him. He may be sick and he may stop breathing again. By this time he will be cold because you could not do three things at once. Priorities are to reduce wind chill and evaporation. Cover him with anything protective.

10 Your observations can be essential to the doctor. Note time of accident, and of any change in condition of casualty. If pulse or breathing rate is taken note this as well. Be ready to give factual information quickly.

If you don't think you would do too well at this, go and learn some first aid.

APPENDIX FOUR

Glossary

ANGLE OF ATTACK: The angle between the chord line of the wing and the airflow. The angle at which the airflow strikes the wing.

ASPECT RATIO: The ratio of wingspan to width (chord) of the wing. A high aspect-ratio wing is narrower than a low aspect-ratio wing. For a parallel chord wing aspect ratio is found by dividing span by the chord; for a complex shape like a rogallo wing it is span^2 divided by area.

BILLOW: The fullness of each half of a rogallo sail when inflated in flight.

CHORD: The width of the wing measured from the leading edge to the trailing edge.

DELTA SAILWING: Any flexible aerofoil hang glider of delta or triangular shape.

FLARE, FLARE OUT, ROUND OUT: The change from a steady descending glide to level flight just above the ground prior to landing; achieved by increasingly raising the nose.

GLIDE RATIO: The ratio between the distance flown and the height lost of a glider in flight, e.g. glide ratio 5 : 1 means that the glider will fly a theoretical distance of 500 m from a height of 100 m.

PITCH: The change in the attitude of a glider in flight, e.g. to pitch up, the nose goes up; to pitch down, the nose goes down.

POLAR: A diagrammatic presentation of performance, giving rate of sink against airspeed.

REFLEX: A reflex aerofoil is one in which the section curves slightly upwards towards the trailing edge. This improves the longitudinal (pitch) stability.

ROGALLO: Generic name for the delta-shape hang glider originated by Francis Rogallo.

ROLL: The movement of a glider when one wing goes up and the other goes down, e.g. in a roll to the left the left wing goes down.

SINK RATE, SINK SPEED: The rate of descent of a glider, e.g. a sink speed of 2 m/sec means that theoretically it will descend to earth at this rate.

SPOILERS: Any external surface which can be deflected into the airflow to create drag.

TIP DRAGGERS: Spoilers, usually vertical, at the wingtips which can be deflected separately to create drag at one wingtip to cause the glider to yaw and turn.

TURNBUCKLES: Another name for bottlescrews. Used to adjust the length of cables.

VENTURI EFFECT: The speeding up of the air as it is drawn through a confined space.

YAW: The skidding or sideways movement of an aircraft when it is not flying through the air in the direction it is pointing.

Index